Ritual

Power, Healing and Community

by Malidoma Patrice Somé

The African Teachings of the Dagara

Swan/Raven & Company ■ Portland, Oregon ■ 1993

1427 N.W. 23rd Ave, Suite 8
Portland, Oregon 97210

(503) 274-1337

These writings, though based on fact, do contain some dialogue and story line that have been modified to better illustrate the purpose of the book or to honor the need of secrecy in the Dagara tradition.

First printing: March 1993

Library of Congress Cataloging-in-Publication Data
Somé, Malidoma Patrice
Ritual: Power, Healing and Community
Series - Echoes of the Ancestors
The African Teachings of the Dagara
Shamanism, Spirituality, African Studies.
pp. 136

ISBN 0-9632310-2-2
1. Shamanism. 2. Spirituality. 3. African Studies.

LC # 92-061258

Cover design and illustration: Marcia Barrentine
Book design by Gary Hardin and Marcia Barrentine

This book was set in 11 point Garamond typeface
Printed in the United States of America

CONTENTS

RITUAL: POWER, HEALING AND COMMUNITY

ACKNOWLEDGMENTS

I give thanks to my own ancestors and to Grandfather Bakhyé, who has maintained a stubborn energetic presence around me, my psyche and my consciousness. He has been persistently injecting me with words, the utterances of which have been very frightening to me, but nonetheless have had tremendous impact on the audiences that have heard them.

I am grateful to the Council of Initiation that ultimately made the decision to initiate me into becoming the kind of person I am. To all the people of my tribe, I am thankful — whether they know me or not, it doesn't matter. For some reason, the more I talk about them, the more I believe in them, the more I can associate with them.

I am grateful to my father, for silently being the kind of support that I always find whenever I am unsure about where to go or what to do.

To all the men who have supported me spontaneously and equally with their trust and belief in the making of the very ritual I describe in this book, I am truly indebted. Without them I would have never known that there is way for one culture to relate to another culture.

I am grateful to Michael Meade for being the "other" tribal African man in a white skin, who through his actions and unspoken words unmistakably has guided me, encouraged me and showed me the way to reach out to men in this frightening white world.

To Robert Bly for being, in many ways, the kind of grandfather that I used to feel comfortable coming close to when I was a child, I honor with admiration and gratefulness.

Robert Moore, who appears to my eyes to be in this culture a man of great spirit, a *boburo* indeed, I embrace with gratitude.

To John Lee for the good things he says to me, and for having acknowledged and confirmed for me thoughts and feelings I was timid or hesitant in conveying — things he suggested or triggered in my own mind by his remarks — I express my thanks.

To James Hillman for his encouragement and support, I express my appreciation. It is his vision and determination that have helped me to move with greater ease within American culture. He has become for me a psychological touchstone to this rapidly changing modern world.

I am grateful again to all the people whom I don't know, who through their very explicit interest in who I am and what I am doing in this country, eventually encouraged me to go ahead and venture into this kind of written disclosure. To them I owe this book, and more.

Series Foreword

*I*s there an understandable reason why contemporary Western culture seems to be deconstructing itself into nihilism and anarchy? Careful reflection based on recent advances in Jungian psychoanalysis can help us to understand some of the primary reasons for our deep — and contagious — disease. *The culture of modernism with its attendant secularization and de-emphasis on the role of ritual in human adaptation has been dominated by the archetype of the magician and its shadow or dysfunctional forms.* One might say that our culture is "possessed" by the immature shadow-magician. When human beings use their magician potentials in the service of healing and community, the deconstructive and sociopathic energies of the immature magician — the trickster — are transformed into a mature, shamanic form that heals both self and the larger community. Traditional tribal cultures sought to transform this energy into the service of human survival and spiritual fulfillment.

I write this forward in Hyde Park in Chicago — a place very near the spot at which the atom was split by a team of sorcerer's apprentices. In the subsequent atomic age we have seen human magician energy harnessed in unprecedented ways to magnify the forces of world deconstruction rather than those of world healing. Can we reverse this misuse of the wonder of the human intellect and imagination?

I believe, with Ewert Cousins, that we are now within reach of an Omega Point in our evolution as a species — that it is now possible for us to begin to reintegrate the wisdom of tribal cultures in the context of a Second Axial Period, a major leap forward in human cultural integration. Cousins sees signs that we might now turn to reaffirm the importance of body, ritual and community — to *reincarnate* magician energy into the embodiment of our species in the context of a viable ecosphere.

If we are to make the turn into a rediscovery of the mature uses of human magician energy, we must learn from traditional tribal cultures. Robert Bly, John Lee and I recently had the privilege of co-leading a conference with Malidoma Somé. We and the other conference participants were deeply touched by Malidoma's stories of ritual leadership and initiatory experience in the tradition of the Dagara tribe. Not only were the stories important and informative, Malidoma's embodiment of mature ritual leadership aided us all in beginning to re-vision what our lives might be like *if we began to use our magician energy for the healing of both individuals and community*. We are extremely fortunate that Malidoma has begun to offer us his wisdom in written form. I have much hope that this series of books by Malidoma will aid us in our attempt to rediscover the mature magician for an inclusive, planetary Earth Community. We *do* have a Shaman within us. Reading these books will help us· understand the healing challenge we face.

ROBERT L. MOORE, PH.D.
JUNGIAN PSYCHOANALYST
HYDE PARK, CHICAGO, ILL.

Robert Moore is a Jungian psychoanalyst and co-author (with Douglas Gillette) of *King, Warrior, Magician, Lover* (HarperCollins); and *The King Within; The Warrior Within; The Magician Within;* and *The Lover Within* (William Morrow). A founder of the Institute for World Spirituality, he is Professor of Psychology and Religion at the Chicago Theological Seminary.

RITUAL
Power, Healing and Community

Introduction

*A*first glimpse can capture an essential aspect of a person. I first saw Malidoma Somé standing in the midst of travelers crowding through an international airport. It was easy to pick him out because his elaborate hat and embroidered cloak were the most commanding garments in sight. The impact of the tribal designs he wore was intensified by the contrast of modern slacks and shoes. The tribal garments display where Malidoma comes from and where his heart still resides. The slacks and shoes show that he is a purposeful traveler in the modern world.

Wearing ceremonial garments in public is not a random act. Rather, it is a ritual statement. The garments are a display of the intention of his tribe to continue to exist, even in the cacophony of the modern world. Malidoma and the Dagara people intend to continue, to weave and embroider life in the intricate way that has been passed to them from their ancestors. The Dagara are dedicated to weaving this world with the Otherworld. The skills of weaving the "other world" of spirits and visions into village life are the same skills Malidoma uses to make pathways between the tribal world and contemporary culture.

Airplanes appear amongst the traditional designs in Malidoma's traveling cloak. It's one of the many surprises that occur around him. Literally and figuratively, he is wearing ancient and modern symbols entwined. His teachings and writings demonstrate a rare ability to introduce tribal wisdom to modern minds. The question is, can the modern world find ways to perceive the subtle knowledge and imagery of the tribal world? Can Western understanding open a place for tribal visions of spiritual life and community rituals to enter?

Malidoma is not a modern person interpreting village life. He's an ancient person interpreting modern life to village elders and showing village ways to modern eyes. Malidoma carries a vision of the tribal world and is able to translate it into Western idioms. I've seen him with a medicine bag made of hide and full of shells in one hand and a laptop computer in the other. He uses each to catch and express the movements of spirit in peoples and places. He is conversant in the languages of modern psychology and comparative literature as well as ancient mythology, healing and divination by shells. He is not the usual traveler, nor the usual observer of either tribal or modern ways. Malidoma is uniquely able to find meaningful pathways in the upheaval that is striking both the tribal world and modern states.

There is no apology in these writings for the reckless imagination, piercing intelligence and intuitive insights jostling in his diviner's bag. There is no willingness to reduce the complexity and surprising nature of the old culture into forms that fit easily into Western beliefs and categories. In order to follow Malidoma into the tribal realm it is necessary to encounter the world of ritual anew. In order to cross the threshold delicately constructed in this series of books, it is necessary to forego the sense that all mysteries can be explained if there's enough time to develop an explanation. It requires letting go of the idea that the world could be known in its entirety if there were just enough electrical wires strung across it. The electricity here comes from invisible wires strung across thresholds into the Otherworld of the ancestors.

Looking through this threshold requires rediscovering the imagination that the West attributes only to children and madmen. In the beginning of the first book of this series, a child wakes in the night startled by a luminous goat studying the sleeping form of his sister. When his fright at this visitation awakens his father, the father sees the same image as the child. The visiting ghost, the visiting goat, is not reduced to a figment or fragment of the child's imagination. Parent and child both see the luminous visitor. The goat leaves a trail that leads through the whole tribe to death and the ancestors. The trouble caused by the goat begins a series of rituals that connect parent, child, grandparent and ancestors. All wind up on the same path attending to the threads of community that are threatened by the spirit in the goat. Everyone is tied one to another by a path of white ash. The rituals that relieve the trouble in the village open the doors to Malidoma's insights into healing in modern societies.

Malidoma Somé is uniquely qualified to find the thresholds between the worlds and hold the gates open. His training in the ancient world and learning in the modern world become a fire of focus because of his willingness to stand where the two collide. The stories within these books have the poignancy of new discoveries as well as the unworn imagination of the ancestors. The commentary has the sharp edge of modern thought and the intricacy which results from the intellect being woven through the ritual complexities of tribal life. The purpose of constructing thresholds that bring this world together is to find the powers that can heal the rends in tribal as well as modern communities.

In Malidoma's piercing observation and ironic speech, you can hear echoes of ages of careful tribal observation. In his descriptions of ritual you can see the shadows and light being played out on the fabric of a village that has maintained pathways to the most ancient sources of human knowledge. Going along this road requires effort, attention to details and delight in the mysterious. Malidoma adds to that a great generosity of spirit and a willingness to lead the way.

— MICHAEL MEADE
VASHON, WASH.
JANUARY 1993

Michael Meade is a teacher, storyteller and writer of mythological tradition. As a musician he is well versed in ethnic music, especially that of Irish heritage. Michael is one of the founders and shapers of the movement addressing the changing role of men in our culture. He is the author of *Men and the Water of Life* (HarperCollins), and co-author with Robert Bly and James Hillman in *The Rag and Bone Shop of the Heart* (HarperCollins).

My Beginnings in Ritual

I was less than three when it happened. The event was so terrifying to me that I felt only Grandfather could protect me. I instinctually sensed the protective power of his knowledge, which only comes with age, as I constantly hid behind him. I could no longer feel safe with just my father.

My father's dwelling was a typical village male's quarters built with earth and finished with cow-dung polish on the inside and outside. My father's house, unlike my mother's, was a two-room building in the compound. The front room opened into the compound yard, a large open space for evening community gatherings. The back room served as a bedroom. On the other side of this open space were my mother's quarters. It was a large oval structure built with mud and wood with extensions on the side that looked like extra-large closets. This windowless wigwamlike lodging was always dark. My mother liked it that way. Every woman in the village liked her dwelling this way. Between these two poles — my father's quarters and my mother's quarters — there was a wall on one side of the open space that linked the two areas together. The wall ended at my father's quarters with a roofless bath and urination facility. On my mother's end of the wall there was a place where she made her clay dishes and jars. On the remaining side of the open space was the kitchen. This is where every evening my mother lit the wood fire to cook the family meal. The ceiling of the kitchen was black with soot and God-knows-what-else. Next to that kitchen was a kind of modest, mud igloo-looking building that attached to my father's quarters. This was where Grandfather lived — apart from everybody else in the compound.

The square look of my father's house with its two rectangular tin windows, perched too high, were the only signs of modernism in the whole compound. Its floor was finished with cow dung mixed with soil collected from the bottom of a riverbed. At night my father liked to sleep with all his children packed on the same bed with him. My mother, who I was quite fond of, slept in her own quarters. She also liked to have her children sleep with her on her straw mat. But her children were also my father's children, and so there was a rule of nightly custody sharing not understood by me to this day. Even though she shared her mat with roaches and worms nursed by the moist dung surface of her room floor, she hated sleeping above the ground. In the village, husband and wife do not share the same bed.

That previous night my sister, my stepbrother and I were sleeping in my father's bedroom. Since sunset, rain had poured from a darkness periodically ripped apart by bright swords of lightning. A terrifying tropical hurricane was in progress.

My father blew out the pale yellow light emanating from the burning shea oil lamp. The ensuing deep darkness forced my eyes closed. I didn't want to sleep. I couldn't. I was scared — scared of the darkness. More than that, I was scared of knowing that I would be awake in such darkness while everyone else slept.

My sister began to snore. She was sleeping next to me at the edge of the common bed. These primitive beds can be a torture to the body. They are hand built with thin pieces of wood from the yila tree, known for growing thin and straight branches. On top of the rectangular surface of wood strips and raw leather a straw mat is laid to diminish the roughness of the

uneven wood. A bed like this is only good for those already won by sleep. You cannot stand being awake on it. Your whole attention turns to avoiding being pinched by your own bed. It didn't take long before I heard someone else snoring. It was my stepbrother. Behind me the regular breathing of my father told me that he too was somewhere in *zanuteg*, the land of sleep. I squeezed my eyes shut. One way or the other I had to get to sleep.

The dark closed in with a hermetic seal. I remained waiting to be freed by sleep. Outside, the hurricane was raging, hurling rain at our mud roof. Rather than focus on the possible destructiveness of this hard rain, my childlike mind chose to remember instead the singing rains. In our village there is nothing more peaceful than lying in bed while rainwater sings its song upon a mud roof. Even the grown-ups like it. There is only concern if the roof begins to leak. Then you have to climb up there in the dark to try and figure out how to seal the hole before the leak becomes like rain itself. Some part of me did not want to sleep unless I could take the singing rain into *zanuteg* with me.

Suddenly, my sister began to talk in her sleep. She was objecting to someone blowing smoke at her. It made no sense to me. I wanted to wake her up, but she was snoring too. Anybody who wakes up a snoring person will catch the snoring disease. I pushed her so she would turn around. Certain sleeping postures are particularly inviting to snoring. I did not want to wake her up, I just wanted to stop her from keeping me awake. Unlike other nights, she continued to talk and snore alternately. Normally she would wake up or at least stop talking for a while. Her persistence intrigued me, so I opened my nearly three-year-old eyes as if to get a better look at what to do about this disease that was robbing me of my sleep. And then I saw it.

Just above my sister's head was a goat sniffing, with its nose moving frenetically as if collecting data. It was luminescent as if its fur were sprinkled with a moon dust as it glowed in the dark. Its horns were branchlike, the likes of which I had never seen before. I did not mind a goat being there. It was not uncommon for domestic animals to roam the compound. The compound was not seen by my people as a place just for human beings. Day in and day out we dealt with domestic animals ambling wherever they pleased to get their needs met. From morning to evening every family compound in the village shared its space with the animals. They are just another thread in the common fabric of community with the Dagara people. There is nothing really new about a goat being in a home. But . . . a goat, awake in the middle of the night, glowing in the dark . . . that was something altogether different. So I screamed.

My father bolted from his sleep ready to scold me for waking the rest. But he was stunned by the vision of the luminescent goat standing in front of him. "What is that?" he asked in a frenzy. The goat made a dash for the narrow exit, missed, and slammed instead into the mud wall. The impact sent it reeling back into my mother's basket of calabashes. The goat fell to its knees, sending the dinnerware and housewares of the basket sprawling across the floor. Still aglow, it then righted itself and dashed through the door into the other room of my father's house. The door that led out into the open space of the compound was closed. The goat leapt at it and disappeared behind the unopened door.

The spectacle was rapid, stunning and noisy. The cacophony of sprawling calabashes, rain pounding on the roof and my sister's screaming at the top of her lungs added to the ensuing confusion. But by that time the goat was nowhere to be seen. My sister clung to me, continuing to scream, while my father swore with each step that crushed another calabash underfoot. He too was trying to find the exit door amidst the total darkness. Or was he trying to find the shea lamp he had earlier extinguished?

The dim yellow light of the shea oil lamp cut through the darkness and revealed the mess of broken calabashes,

earthenware, sun-baked clay and kilned pots everywhere. The shiny ebony color of the broken clay dispersed throughout the bedroom spelled loss. Through them, I could hear my mother's chagrin. These were all her possessions. The brown calabashes were not all broken into pieces. Some had survived the chaos, but one could see the cracks they had sustained. The mixture of calabashes and clay was plain evidence of some tumultuous activity that had taken place. Father walked out of the room, lamp in hand, once again leaving us in darkness. I could not stand it. I hurriedly followed right behind him into the other room. My sister followed suit. Father was looking for the ill-fated goat. It was nowhere to be seen. He searched each of the two rooms of his mud suite while my sister and I tagged closely behind him.

Shortly after dawn, Father decided to call Grandfather in. It didn't take Grandfather long to spy a thin line of coagulated blood running from the bed where we had slept through the whole bedroom, into the other room, up the wooden downspout, onto the roof of my father's suite into the openness outside. Grandfather was not pleased as his face seemed cooked in disappointment. His gloomy attitude indicated that something other than a simple goat had visited us during the night.

Grandfather then returned to his own room. The rest of his day was spent divining the source of the previous night's mystery. Everyone heard about the story of the goat sniffing at my sister during the stormy night before. The family compound was crowded with people who had heard the news, curiosity seekers and people who offered their help if there was something to be done. But nothing happened that day. Grandfather had lain a thin line of ash along every door of the house. Other than that there was nothing special going on that I could see. However, the next morning my stepbrother began to feel ill. He stayed in bed. Later, blood began streaming from his nose and his mouth. He died at sunset.

The funeral ceremony that followed was full of agitation. At the instruction of Grandfather, any person entering the

ceremonial space was checked with different talismanic objects. Of course I wondered why. Surely this was not an ordinary funeral ritual. The principal participants in the funeral ceremony, my father, mother and some uncles and cousins I knew little about, had all painted their bald heads with white paint. This was to be a strategic grief ceremony.

In the afternoon of the second day, Grandfather, who had not come out once since the beginning of the ceremony, appeared with several others his age. The musicians stopped playing their xylophones. The wailers and mourners slowly grew quieter. The crowd became silent with anticipation. One of the old men accompanying Grandfather spoke to the crowd about murder, crime and upcoming punishment, about decay of order and community. He said something about evil whose very good is the bad done to society. I understood from his statements that someone was responsible for the sudden death of my stepbrother, though I could not link this to the goat that had visited a couple of nights before.

From that day on, this strange event left me feeling Grandfather's protection around me. It was as if some secret existed between us — some secret that was never to be spoken. Twenty years went by before I remembered to ask what really happened. I was told that my stepbrother's death had been the work of a witch. That was taken for granted since no one can enter even the doorless homes of the village without a little bit of knowledge in transmogrify or shape-shifting. All homes of the village are protected by spiritual ancestors and by specific juju hidden at the entrance. This particular witch was able to enter our house because my father had an outstanding debt to the Earth Shrine for nearly ten years. This debt was to have been paid through a ritual. The delay (or refusal to acquit himself) for what he owed had resulted in the weakening of the protective family shield. And the evildoer took advantage of this.

However, the witch died that same year following the strategic grief ceremony. My father told me that the only way

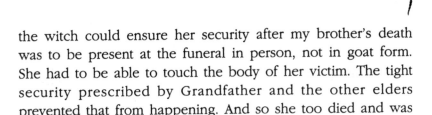
the witch could ensure her security after my brother's death was to be present at the funeral in person, not in goat form. She had to be able to touch the body of her victim. The tight security prescribed by Grandfather and the other elders prevented that from happening. And so she too died and was buried inside an anthill with no funeral ceremony.

My father finally performed the ritual that he owed to the Earth Shrine, but the questions remain: Why do the innocent suffer from the negligence of others? Why is it that social responsibilities are inseparable from rituals? And why is it so important that every individual in a community stay in good rapport with their gods and goddesses?

Here was a ritual, a benign ceremonial offering, that was supposed to have been done ten years before the fatality of my stepbrother. In spite of his death, the ritual owed to the Earth Shrine still had to be performed in order to prevent more catastrophe, not to address the catastrophe itself.

This story shows that, as in many societies, ritual occupies a unique place among the Dagara. They are a people whose life is determined by what the natural forces in the world require of them. Spread throughout the arid region of present northern Ghana, southern Burkina Faso and the Ivory Coast, this tribe is known by others as the Tribe of Concealment and Magic. The life of the tribe is regulated by the tropical climate of the area composed of two seasons: the rainy season and the dry season. The rainy season runs invariably from April, May or June to September or October. During this time, farming activity occupies the lives of the people. They practice subsistence agriculture, which is very dependent upon the amount of rain that falls in any farming season. Everybody grows millet, ground nuts, corn and beans. The lengthy remainder of the year is dry and idle. People use that time either to emigrate to the city to seek jobs, or to stay in the villages. Those who stay in the villages experiment with medicine, do initiation and practice ritual. Storytelling, drumming, dancing and singing are practiced during the dry season.

For the Dagara, ritual is, above all else, the yardstick by which people measure their state of connection with the hidden ancestral realm, with which the entire community is genetically connected. In a way, the Dagara think of themselves as a projection of the spirit world. It is composed of the world of the ancestors, the place where the dead go to rest, the world of spirits where non-human entities in charge of the order of nature dwell. They are also a part of the in-between world where supernatural realities, such as medicine, transmogrify and witchcraft percolate into the natural world.

I have chosen to speak about ritual first in this series of books because the abandonment of ritual can be so devastating. From the spiritual viewpoint, ritual is inevitable and necessary if one is to live. The death of my stepbrother is symbolic of how spirits "think," that is, how they view their relationship with humans on a cosmic scale. The young ones are the future of the old ones. To allow this future to happen, the old ones must work with the Otherworld. When an elder fails to perform his work with respect to the spiritual, the future of this elder is threatened, not the present. Where ritual is absent, the young ones are restless or violent, there are no real elders, and the grown-ups are bewildered. The future is dim.

The Dimensions of Ritual

In tribal communities, such as the Dagara, there are several dimensions to ritual. There is communal ritual, where every grown-up member of the village is obliged to attend. These gatherings take care of the village's need to reaffirm its unity under one spirit, be it Tigan the Earth Shrine, Dawera, the Nature Shrine, or Namwin, the Supreme God.

There is family ritual, which can be a subcommunity honoring of certain spirits in the name of family unity or for other reasons. It is community ritual that allows these isolated

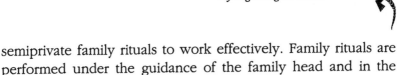

semiprivate family rituals to work effectively. Family rituals are performed under the guidance of the family head and in the presence of every responsible family member. Any initiated person is considered responsible and must attend family rituals.

From the family rituals and, in a way, from community rituals, there are derived individual rituals. My father's failure in honoring of the Earth Shrine is an example of individual ritual that had affect on more than just the individual. It eventually affected the family and the community. Individual rituals are just as important as family rituals and community rituals. This means that these rituals are interdependent even though they look separate. Likewise, a ritual performed by a community liberates a certain energy that makes it possible for other rites to happen at a family and individualistic level.

These ritualistic hierarchies are not designed at random. When the yearly village rituals are not performed, other rituals suffer with ineffectiveness. Ten years ago, the whole village suffered drought because the priest of the Earth Shrine had passed away, leaving his first son to carry on the priestly tradition. But this son either forgot or refused to perform this fundamental rite. It should be noted that the priest of the Earth Shrine is usually seen as a collective person. Whatever he does, alone or in the presence of the village, is considered communal. So if he fails to do anything, the community suffers.

Families gathered to carry on with their family rituals and individuals complied with individual ritual, but disaster resulted anyway. Many died in the drought including the new priest of the Earth Shrine. Individual duty in ritual cannot take the place of communal duty and vice versa.

My grandfather could not perform the ritual that my father owed to the Earth Shrine because his task was to take care of the family rituals in order to render individual rituals possible. We all owe to the cosmic order, and it is impossible, at this level, to do for others what others are expected to do for themselves. We owe to the cosmic order because we are individually and communally responsible for its maintenance.

Every person is sent to this outpost called earth to work on a project that is intended to keep this cosmic order healthy. Any person that fails to do what he or she must do energetically stains the cosmic order.

It may be too soon to say that the ills of American culture come from a situation similar to that which lead to the death of my stepbrother or the famine ten years ago. But I am tempted to think that when the focus of everyday living displaces ritual in a given society, social decay begins to work from the inside out. The fading and disappearance of ritual in modern culture is, from the viewpoint of the Dagara, expressed in several ways: the weakening of links with the spirit world, and general alienation of people from themselves and others. In a context like this there are no elders to help anyone remember through initiation of his or her important place in the community. Those who seek to remember have an attraction toward violence. They live their life constantly upset or angry, and those responsible for them are at a loss as to what to do.

For an African who comes to America, there are no words to describe the shock he encounters. At first blush this culture shows itself as heaven somewhere away from the planet. But there is still connection to the planet in a left-handed way. Americans are spoiled every which way, to the point where they behave as if no one else on the planet can possibly be hungry or unsheltered or without a television set or a telephone. Incredibly, I find that they are even aware that they are the only people in this whole world to enjoy the privilege of waste and squandering. If an American isn't expressing pity for a person who doesn't have a television or telephone, he's expressing excitement at the thought of how enjoyable it would be to witness a tribesman being introduced to these modern gadgets. Sometimes they even expect the rest of the world still to be walking naked, sheltered in huts and eating lizards and worms.

I remember once being asked by an American, "Does everyone in your country still sleep in trees?" And I replied,

"Yes." He was overjoyed (or at least seemed so) at meeting someone who had slept in a tree. But when I added that in our capital city of Ouagadougou the ambassador of the United States sleeps in the tallest tree, he walked away confused and a bit suspicious. Americans are bred to expect the rest of the world to be underdeveloped.

The Dagara people, on the other hand, are suspicious of abundance. It translates into a cultural attitude that a person of abundance is a person too worldly to deal with hardship. This is an obvious trick from a god to put someone to sleep before the final blow. In my village there was a man whom everyone knew to be very poor, or at least he did not have anything that anyone would desire. His compound was as normal as anyone else's. He was married with several children. But one day the man began to act most strangely. First, there was delivery of a half-dozen cows from nearby Ghana by someone no one knew of. The man soon began to build a modern home and bought himself a brand new English bicycle. He wore clean clothes. He had changed in ways that were suspicious. And he showed abundance in ways that insulted the entire setup of the tribe. People waited for the inevitable. It occurred quickly.

The man's oldest son died mysteriously. He was drowned in the shallow waters of the river. It did not take long before one of his daughters passed away while asleep. But this was not the worst. He killed his wife accidentally by letting a beam fall on her. Very soon the man became a maniac, stealing from people things he did not even need, such as food and dirty clothes. People he stole from knew what he did but never indicted him. His own end came when he self-destructed.

The only place where abundance is warranted is in nature. A person who wastes is a person who insults the gods. In light of the waste encountered in the modern world, one wonders if anyone knows that there is a world outside of this abundance where people are aware of priorities other than materialism.

The greatest shock that American culture has on traditional people is its notion of speed. My role in our village is to be a translator to my elders of modern culture and a translator to modern culture of my people's ways. I remember a social moment spent around millet beer where I began to speak about the notion of motion. Millet beer is brewed by women. First, millet is germinated and dried in the sun. Then it is ground and boiled heavily to extract the juice. This juice is boiled again for a whole day to ensure its fermentation, then cooled to ambient temperature. By the time it is fermented, the entire process has taken about three days. It is around a calabash of this beer that people socialize. As they say in the village, "One drinks his way to interesting talk," or, "The spirit of millet beer is generous in words." In the conversation, I pointed to a circle of old people who were sitting around enjoying the day and explained that such stillness would be a shock to a person in the West, whose schedule is much faster. One of the elders asked, "Where do these white people run to every morning?"

"To their workplaces, of course."

"Why do they have to run to something that is not running away from them?"

"They do not have time." I had to say this word in French because there is no equivalent in the local language. The conversation came to a halt when the elder had to ask what this "time" was.

Among the Dagara, the absence of "time" generates a mode of life whose focus is on the state of one's spirit. This is not comparable to what machine-dominated culture is all about. While in America, the newcomer thinks at first that people move hurriedly in order to enjoy the thrill of speed. But a more traditional look at motion, at speed, quickly reveals that speed is not necessarily so much a movement toward something as it is a movement away from something.

The elder who noticed that moderns don't have to run toward something that isn't moving was pointing to the idea that to move is also to keep oneself distracted. The indigenous mind cannot conceive of it otherwise. And so the elder sees

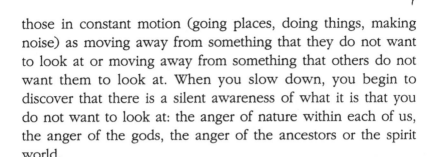

those in constant motion (going places, doing things, making noise) as moving away from something that they do not want to look at or moving away from something that others do not want them to look at. When you slow down, you begin to discover that there is a silent awareness of what it is that you do not want to look at: the anger of nature within each of us, the anger of the gods, the anger of the ancestors or the spirit world.

In his book *The Africans*, Ali Mazrui began his study of the triple heritage of the African people by pointing out that the ills of the continent of Africa nowadays are the result of the anger of the ancestors in the face of the general desecration brought about by modernism. He indicates that throwing away one's culture for another is an insult to the dead, and can result, as in the case of Africa, in a lot of unresolved ills. In a way, Mr. Mazrui is not just speaking about mechanized Africa, where the worship of the ancestors is being gradually replaced with the worship of machines. He is also speaking to the developed countries, where the antlike frenzy of life, characterized by a work-obsessed culture, is symptomatic of an illness that is perhaps too large to face.

Thus speed is a way to prevent ourselves from having to deal with something we do not want to face. So we run from these symptoms and their sources that are not nice to look at. To be able to face our fears, we must remember how to perform ritual. To remember how to perform ritual, we must slow down.

I believe that the difference between the indigenous world and the industrial world has mostly to do with speed — not about whether one world needs to have ritual and the other doesn't. In light of what I said earlier, it appears that the indigenous world looks while the industrial world overlooks.

Indigenous people are indigenous because there are no machines between them and their gods. There are no machines barring the door to the spirit world where one can enter in and listen to what is going on within at a deep level, participating in the vibration of Nature. Where machines speak in place of gods, people are hard put to listen, even more hard put to vibrate with the realm of Nature.

Thus the two worlds of the traditional and the industrial are diametrically opposed. The indigenous world, in trying to emulate Nature, espouses a walk with life, a slow, quiet day-to-day kind of existence. The modern world, on the other hand, steams through life like a locomotive, controlled by a certain sense of careless waste and destruction. Such life eats at the psyche and moves its victims faster and faster along, as they are progressively emptied out of their spiritual and psychic fuel. It is here, consequently, where one's spirit is in crisis, that speed is the yardstick by which the crisis itself is expressed.

Any person in modern culture who is aware of this destruction from the machine world upon the spiritual world of the individual realizes that there is a starvation of the soul. And realizing that, he or she starts to wonder what to do about it. In places that I have been to speak to people about the beliefs and realities of the indigenous world, there has been a consistent number of people who have been so touched, even profoundly shaken by what I was telling them that I have to believe that I was not so much appealing to their minds as I was awakening something within their souls — something that has always been there. This tells me that there must be an indigenous person within each of us.

This indigenous archetype within the modern soul is an archetype that is in serious need of acknowledgment within the person. A different set of priorities dwells there, a set of priorities long forgotten in higher cultures. People in touch with this archetype are in search of caring, for their spirit seeks to transcend the stress placed on the body and the mind by the rapid motion of everyday life around them. Such people would not be ashamed to express their hunger for transcendence — these are the kind of people in need of ritual.

Ritual: The Anti-Machine

Ritual in a way is an anti-machine, even though the industrial world is not totally devoid of the practice of ritual. David Kertzer, in *Ritual, Politics and Power*, points out it is innately inscribed within humans to do ritual. He goes on to show that ritual exists in every aspect of political practice where the construction of power is ordered by symbol and ceremony. For him, ritual is unavoidable in modern political and social interplay because it is something that enables people to deal with archetypes. There is some truth in such a vision. But I think that the term is being manipulated to fit certain urges for legitimization.

A spirit can be used to legitimize someone's desires. For example, someone can say that a spirit told him or her to do something, which legitimizes his or her unwarranted action (as in the American comedy line "The devil made me do it!"). One can claim divine sponsorship to justify actions that have nothing to do with the divine. One has only to look at American televangelism for that.

It is not possible, similarly, to associate the hasty, grinding wheels of the machine culture as the echoes or soundings of ritual. *Ritual is not compatible with the rapid rhythm that industrialism has injected into life.* So whenever ritual happens in a place commanded by or dominated by a machine, ritual becomes a statement against the very rhythm that feeds the needs of that machine. It makes no difference whether it is a political machine or otherwise.

I say this because it feels to me that this elusive sense of the divine in the modern world and the practice of blatant consumerism have spread even into the spiritual realm. This reveals the attempt of a mechanized culture to protect itself from having to face even subtle duties toward its higher self. To say that ritual is needed in the industrialized world is an understatement. We have seen in my own people that it is probably impossible to live a sane life without it.

In the face of the sweeping industrial imperialism wrought upon the continent of Africa by Europeans, the traditional African, in general, and the Dagara in particular, have been unable to conceive of a way to respond to the attractiveness of the machinelike world without abandoning their ancestral ways. Progress brings a different world into the already existing world of the indigenous person. In Africa, whoever gets "touched" by progress is superficially in two worlds: the traditional and the corporate.

The corporate world dims the light of the traditional world by exerting a powerful magnetic shadowlike pull on the psyche of the individual. Thus the individual feels compelled to respond. But as he or she tries to respond, the individual begins to realize that the source of the pull is elusive. For the machine world either refuses to provide a sense of complete satiation or it just doesn't have it to provide. And yet the machine world cannot let go of the individual (or else the machine will cease its motion) in spite of the fact that it cannot fully provide for the individual's needs. So one of the ways to maintain a certain sense of self is to remain somewhat linked to essential traditionalism.

This is made apparent every time there is a death in one of our cities. The immediate instinct is to carry the body back to the village in order that a proper mourning ritual can happen. People of the same village within the city will gather to prepare whatever is needed for the journey back home. They bring the funeral home, as they say nowadays. These kinds of funerals account for 10 percent of all the funerals celebrated in the villages.

The city dweller in Africa who works for a company does so to meet his basic needs as a human being. His adherence to a machine culture does not have the power to disconnect him fully from the roots of his ancestry. Very few sever themselves from home. Periodic adherence to proscribed rituals while dwelling in this industrialized culture is the medicine with which to dress the wounds and repair the deformities brought

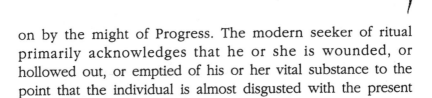

on by the might of Progress. The modern seeker of ritual primarily acknowledges that he or she is wounded, or hollowed out, or emptied of his or her vital substance to the point that the individual is almost disgusted with the present state of his or her life.

These wounds are evidence of the need to enter into a special creative process. They are the language with which entry into the realm of ritual is possible. As long as one does not deploy special energy to repress and deny these wounds, but rather contains them creatively — that is, in ritual — then one is working on oneself as a potential survivor of the holocaust and the tyranny of Progress. I mean to say that the hurt that a person feels in the midst of this modern culture should be taken as a language spoken to himself or herself by the body. And the meaning of such a language is found in doing something about the part of oneself that is not acknowledged.

Pain and Ritual

Human senses are devices of communication. Sight is a language, as are pain, touch, smell and taste. The most powerful among them is the feeling of pain. For the Dagara elder, pain is the result of a resistance to something new — something toward which an old dispensation is at odds. We are made of layers of situations or experiences. Each one of them likes to use a specific part of ourselves in which to lodge. It's like a territory. A new experience that does not have a space to sit in within us will have to kick an old one out. The old one that does not want to leave will resist the new one, and the result is registered by us as pain. This is why the elders call it *Tuo*. It means invasion, hunting, meeting with a violent edge. It also means boundary. Pain, therefore, is our body complaining about an intruder. Body complaint is understood as the soul's language relayed to us. A person in pain is being spoken to by that part of himself that knows only how to communicate in this way.

Thus, when an initiated member of the community registers communication through pain, it is a signal that the soul is in need of some communion with its spiritual counterpart. In other words, the soul is moving old furniture out and bringing in new furniture. Whether that eventually works out well is another question. We do not always allow ourselves to work through pain. More often than not, we think pain is a signal that we must stop, rather than find its source. Our souls do not like stagnation. Our souls aspire toward growth, that is, toward remembering all that we have forgotten due to our trip to this place, the earth. In this context, a body in pain is a soul in longing. To shut down the pain is to override the call of the soul. When this happens it is a repressive measure taken against oneself, which has somber consequences.

Is it possible then to say that pain is good, primarily because it is a call to growth? The Dagara elders would say yes. They believe that a person who has suffered is a person who has heard pain (*won Tuo*). The person hears the pain as a creative action, connecting that person with his or her highest self, which prescribes an alternative to spiritual death. So pain at least teaches us something. It is commotion, e-motion and a call for a rebirth. It teaches that one must return to a mode of living that began with life itself. And it draws from nature and the cosmos life-essence that seeks to align itself with the existing powers.

Such living is what ancient tribes have adopted for thousands of years. And its success can be seen in the fact that in it there is room for the entire person to exist. This means that the world of progress with its all-consuming tendencies is an essentialist that feeds on anything that lives, turning the human into an indentured servant fed with things material, yet starved for everything else. In this context, ritual is this return to the ancient with a plea for help directed to the world of the spirit.

Ritual, Ceremony and Us

G randfather! Stop that! You're tickling me. What is that?"
I squealed. Grandfather wouldn't let me turn and see
what he was up to. It was another one of his "lessons."

"Brother Malidoma, be still. Tell me what is happening."

Since I was very young at the time, I don't recall what led
up to this exercise. But how I remember the shrill peeping of a
little chick as Grandfather rubbed its wet downy body against
mine. I squirmed at the tickling sensations, but Grandfather
held me tight to keep me from looking around.

"Grandfather, you are tickling me with a little chick. Why
are you tickling me?"

"I am not tickling you," he promised. Grandfather was
trying to teach me something about ritual. I screamed with
laughter once again, unable to contain myself. Was Grandfather
lying?

"Grandfather, why are you tickling me?"

"I'm not tickling you."

"Yes you are."

"But I am not, brother Malidoma." How did this relate to
ritual? "Look," he explained, "we are doing what we are doing
so as to learn how to play with the spirits. They are at the
heart of ritual."

With his grip lessening, I turned to ask, "Why do people do rituals?" I could see no baby chick. "They kill chickens, goats and all kinds of animals, and they eat some and throw others away. Why?" Grandfather never looked at anybody while answering a question. He was working on a tobacco pouch while he spoke.

"Do you know why you go to the bathroom? Do you know why you urinate?"

"Of course I know. I can't help it."

"Well then, you know why we do rituals."

Village life rotates around subsistence activities (farming and hunting) and the practice of ritual. In a way, subsistence work links humans together while ritual links humans to the gods or God. Living with my parents throughout my university years, it felt like the dead were not really dead. At least once a day we had something to say to our ancestors. At least once a day a word is addressed to the shrine of Nature, be it at home before undertaking a journey to the farm or to another village, be it in the farm before working at it.

The presence of the Otherworld is never trivial. The general impression is that ritual should precede human involvement with the world and with each other. Thus planting begins with the offering of a sample of that which is going to be planted. In a way, the planting already happens at a divine level before happening actually. When one goes on a journey, be it into the city or be it to the nearby village, one must ritualize the travel at the ancestral shrine prior to undertaking the journey itself. It is assumed that, at the end of the ritual, in the course of which the traveler gives himself away to the gods, the journey itself has already happened in a metaphoric world. The rest is just translation of metaphor. When a person is suddenly sick, while he lies in pain, the head of the house first goes to a diviner and finds out what went wrong. There he finds out what ritual must be done. He comes back home, finds the elements that must enter into the ritual and performs

it. Only after all this does it finally become necessary to do something directly with the sick person. By that time, the illness has been dealt with symbolically. What remains is the actualization of that which has already been performed.

It follows then that primitive cultures normally deal with the physical world at the last stage. What goes wrong in the visible world is only the tip of the iceberg. So to correct a dysfunctional state of affairs effectively, one must first locate its hidden area, its symbolic dimension, work with it first, and then assist in the restoration of the physical (visible) extension of it. Visible wrongs have their roots in the world of the spirit. To deal only with their visibility is like trimming the leaves of a weed when you mean to uproot it. Ritual is the mechanism that uproots these dysfunctions. It offers a realm in which the unseen part of the dysfunction is worked on in ways that affect the seen.

Consequently, each time we enter a ritual space we do so because something in the physical world has warned us of possible deterioration at hand. This presupposes that one does not enter into a ritual without a *purpose*, a goal. As I said earlier, ritual is called for because our soul communicates things to us that the body translates as need, or want, or absence. So we enter into ritual in order to respond to the call of the soul. So illness, perhaps, is the sign language of the soul in need of attention. This means that our soul is the part of us that picks up on situations well ahead of our conscious awareness of them. Purpose is the driving force that contributes to the effectiveness of ritual.

In the village, there are rituals that can backfire on the person performing them. These rituals do not have a purpose and thereby turn against the performer. This is tricky, because one would assume that any ritual done to heal must be good. Elders say that ritual is like an arrow shot at something. When the intended target is not there, the arrow invents one. In such cases, the target may simply be a positive manifestation, but it could also be a negative manifestation. Take, for example, a case in which someone sacrifices a chicken prior to a journey instead of pouring a libation. The chicken sacrifice has the ability of righting a wrongdoing. In this case of the journey, no wrongdoing existed. Because of that, the person would meet trouble along the way because that person had set himself or herself up for it. It is like taking pills for a headache when you are fine, and ending up with a stomach ache because of it. So in such a case, the ritual is just misdirected.

I still remember to this day a ritual involving the sacrifice of a chicken that died belly-down instead of belly-up. It was in the course of one of my returns home. The diviner I saw the day after my homecoming said that the spirit of my grandfather was angry at me because I had been using his name abroad without any concrete initiative showing that I really did care for him. I was told that I should atone for the anger with the sacrifice of three chickens. I was uneasy about the whole situation because I had never thought that the spirit of my grandfather could be mad at me for any reason. Nonetheless, I felt that I should do what I was told since it would be a long time before I returned to the village again.

In the village, sacrifices are very common. They fix things already gone wrong. And since there is always a plethora of things going wrong on a daily basis, chickens, goats, sheep and even cows were instrumental in taking care of ritual requirements. The chicken died belly-down. My father and I took the bloody knife used to cut its throat to the nearby diviner. The divination now revealed that the spirit of my grandfather had not wanted atonement, but solidification of our friendship and kinship. This is not something that requires blood at all. Spirits, like animals, do not take more than they need. My grandfather did not need any chicken so he would not accept it. Instead he wanted a little bit of ash and water to ensure the continuity of both his protection and his love. It was that simple, but a chicken had been wasted already. So we went back home, did what we were told by killing another chicken to repair the damage done by killing the previous one for the wrong reason. Of course it meant an interesting occasion for a barbecue. There are cases when the sacrificed animal cannot be eaten. One of them involves the prevention of death. The animal in this case is either buried or abandoned in the wild.

Ritual is also imposed on us by our souls even though we can still prevail upon our souls for rituals. In other words, ritual can happen without someone feeling pain. In this case it is either a preventive ritual or a celebration ritual. Among the Dagara, a good harvest must be celebrated with the gods. The whole village chooses one day in the course of which samples of harvest are brought to the gods along with sacrifices of chickens and goats. This ritual offering is followed by a feast that translates the human expression of oneness with the divine. Consequently, the purpose of this ritual is to avoid having to face a later ritual oriented around pain. This means that when one cruises with the world of the spirits, rituals are less and less a matter of stopping commotions than they are a matter of maintaining a healthy state of balance. Yet, to arrive at that level of harmony, one must stay in the correct practice of ritual for a lengthy period of time.

As alluded to earlier, the success of a ritual depends on the purpose of the individuals involved with it. Any ritual designed to satisfy an ego is a ritual for show, and therefore is a spiritual farce. But any ritual in which the persons involved invite the spirits to come and help in something that humans are not capable of handling by themselves or in which humans honor gift-giving from the divine, there is a likelihood of the ritual working.

Some years ago I was involved in a burial rite in the capital city of Ouagadougou, Burkina Faso, in Western Africa. An old woman was dead and there was no way to take the body back to the village for her funeral. There were three or four of us who had been asked to dig the grave. It was late in the evening when we went to the municipal cemetery and began

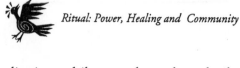
digging while people gathered silently at the house of the deceased. Toward midnight the grave was almost finished, and I was very exhausted. The dew had fallen on the grass, and its coolness numbed the nerves and increased my desire to rest. So while my co-workers were finishing the job, I moved a few yards away to take a catnap in the tall grass. When I awoke I found the cemetery all lit up. It was like daytime, and there were people everywhere. I figured it was the burial entourage that had accompanied the body while I had slept. It didn't take too long for me to notice that there was something odd about them. They were all dressed up with long ceremonial robes. All of them wore hats, and each sat on a grave, which I found intriguing. Fear crept into my very bones. I began to feel cold and numb. I thought about screaming, for I knew what was going on. My mind worked fast as I decided to get the hell out of there. But as I stood to leave, each of the grave-sitters also stood one after the other. Thoughts raced through my mind anew. What if I made some noise? I dismissed that, thinking no one would hear me, and even if they did no one in their right mind would come near this place. I was alone — living flesh among a graveyard of ghosts.

The attention of each ghostly figure was undivided toward me. I looked at the perimeter of the cemetery, where I could see the sourceless light ending into the dark of night. It wasn't far away, I thought, and began to walk toward the darkness. They all began to follow me. I knew that I was not supposed to look back. The intensity of their presence behind me was such that every step took an eternity. I could not run. Each leg weighed a ton. What made the walk possible I will never know. I felt half-paralyzed. The challenge to lift each leg and place it in front of the other was overwhelming. My back felt like a burning platform fueled by a voracious, consuming energy that seemed to be eating away at me. This slowed me even more. On top of that, I didn't know if I was frightened, in pain, or just indifferent. All I knew was that I was witnessing something unearthly. I was in the wrong place at the wrong time, and I had no idea what was going to happen next.

As I approached the edge of night, the pull from behind increased. It was awful to sense from behind me a huge uproar coming from hundreds of throats, distant yet very close. It seemed like I was the only one intended to hear it. Never was darkness more appealing to me as at that moment when I was about to enter it. The closer I got the lighter my body seemed to become and the faster I was able to pursue it. I literally jumped that last few feet into the city night air. It felt as if I had been released from a powerful magnetic force as I ran toward the street light. Behind me I could still sense a force field following. Either I was dragging it or I was simply being pushed by it as if it were giving me wings.

When I arrived home at my apartment it was a little after four A.M. My body was on fire; I was sweating and shivering all over from the combination of fever and exhaustion. Until daylight finally arrived, I felt suspended between life and death with reality filtering through imprecisely. For a while, it seemed as though I were back at the cemetery. It was impossible to sleep, for every time I closed my eyes I would see the graveyard all lit up again by the sourceless light, crowded with people mesmerized by my presence, wanting to come closer to me.

At noon, one of the friends who had helped dig the grave with me came to visit. He was stunned to see how ill I was. I told him the whole story. He was in tears as he told me that I slept in the cemetery for nearly five hours. The old lady had been buried around midnight, and everyone had left quickly. The tall grass had hidden me from people, so no one saw me. And they, thinking that I had woken up when the burial began, did not even check to see if I was in the crowd. My friend suggested that I go home to my village. Phenomena like this cannot be endured without first checking them out with ancestral understanding. I, too, knew I needed to get back to my village home. Feeling weaker and weaker and fighting against a constant drift into hallucination, I knew I was a mess. My friend decided to go out and look for transportation that would get me back to my village. In the middle of the afternoon he finally returned, having found nothing. He offered to take me to the central station and put me on any truck going the general direction of my village. I accepted.

When I reached home, it was almost dawn. From afar, I saw someone sitting on the tip of the roof looking in my direction. As I came closer, I noticed it was my father. I knew he knew it was I. But he asked anyway, "Is that you, Malidoma?"

"Yes, father, it is," I gasped.

"Praise be to the ancestors," he volunteered as he came down from the compound roof. We didn't even shake hands. I felt like I was beyond recognition.

I woke up my uncle and cousin. An hour later I was in the ancestral room facing the shrine of the dead in the total darkness. The ancestral room is usually a healing and ritual shrine installed in a hidden windowless room inside the compound. My uncle prayed to the shrine, then asked my stepbrother to bring in the black sheep. He poured water on the animal while speaking about death and life. Then, my father, who held a chicken in his hand, spoke. He thanked the spirits of the family for saving my life by directing me to come home. Then he plunged the screaming chicken into the water and ran it up and down my body clockwise. Each time the chicken came into contact with me, its feathers produced a strange sensation. I held my breath, closed my eyes and focused on the image of the cemetery under daylight in the middle of the night. The image faded each time the chicken came into contact with my body. Suddenly, I noticed that the chicken was struggling for life. My father threw it away. It yelled, darted upward and crashed to the floor of the medicine room — dead. I was then asked to sit on the back of the sheep while it was decapitated.

By the time all of this was completed, it was almost daylight. I went into the compound and, for the first time since the "nap" in the cemetery, slept. When I woke up that afternoon, my father was sitting next to me. In fact it was his presence that woke me. He told me that several people had seen me entering and leaving the homes of relatives. They knew something had happened to me and that my soul was out of my body. The worst of it was that if I did not come home physically within two days I would be dead. There was apparently no way to alert me to the fact that I should rush home for the very ritual that had just been performed. The village is so isolated from the outside world that it is utterly impossible to rush anything back and forth. So my father made a pledge to the ancestors. He promised them a cow if they could figure out a way to get me home within the next twenty-four hours so that I could be reunited with my spirit. I told my father what had happened in the cemetery. For him it was all too clear. The sight of the spirits of the dead ripped my spirit away from me. No one survives the glance of a dead person. Because I was, in a sense, already dead, only the death of something else would save me from actual death. This is what happened with the chicken and the sheep. It still took me a week to regain my strength. Although this was not the last time something like this happened, I never forgot it. It took the death ritual to save me from death. The blood of an animal prevented another human from having to be put into the ground.

Our Role in Ritual

The episode in the graveyard is an extreme example that illustrates what actually happens when one is urgently in need of ritual. How many souls wander aimlessly out of their bodies, unconnected? How many people are gripped by the hand of death when it is still possible to loosen its grasp? To be in a machinelike culture is to have one's soul constantly at risk of being sucked out.

When sacrifice is the only way to save a person from death, or, as I have come to notice in this culture, from fatal psychic or physical disruption — auto accidents, psychological illness, stress or depression — how does one find ritual space or sacred space when everywhere around no one seems to be aware that some kind of sacrificial ritual is needed? There are many cases in which people live separated from their souls in this culture. There are many cases of people actually ending their lives because there was no home to go to nor any kind of ritual to receive, such as the one from which I was fortunate enough to benefit.

A Dagara elder would include such situations as accidents, heart attacks, or any sudden death within the category of separated souls. So the question as to whether an accident could have been avoided has its answer linked to whether it is possible for society to see the soul of the dying before its actual death.

So ritual draws from this area of human existence where the spirit plays a life-giving role. We do not make miracles, we speak the kind of language that is interpreted by the supernatural world as a call to intervene in a stabilizing way in a particular life. Consequently, our role in ritual is to be human. We take the initiative to spark a process, knowing that its success is not in our hands but in the hands of the kind of forces we invoke into our lives. So the force field we create within a ritual is something coming from the spirit, not something coming from us. We are only instruments in this kind of interaction between dimensions, between realms.

There is ritual each time a spirit is called to intervene in human affairs. The structure of the ritual is what I would like to call ceremony because it can vary from time to time and from place to place. So a ceremony, perhaps, is the anatomy of a ritual. It shows what actually is taking place in the visible world, on the surface, and can therefore be seen, observed, corrected. The invisible part of the ritual, that which actually happens as a result of the ceremony, is what carries the ritual quality within itself. In my case, the killing of the chicken and the sheep along with being brought into sacred or ritual space,

the ancestral shrine, are ceremonial. Becoming well after that is the effect of the ritual imbedded in the ceremony.

In the ritual, one has to have participants who are invisible and can actually produce a result that is unexpected. And because we take the risk or the initiative of putting a request to the spirits to intervene in our affairs, their coming turns our activity (ceremony) into a ritual. It still means that we as individuals play a central role in making a ritual happen. The gods themselves will not enact the ritual without us. What actually makes ritual a requirement is far beyond what the world, as it is, can handle. In the surface world our ability to make things happen is very limited. This limitation is a reflection of the incompleteness of a world without the spirit realm. So Spirit is our channel through which every gap in life can be filled. But the spirit realm will not take care of these gaps without our conscious participation. Thus our collaboration makes us central to the actual happening of a ritual.

The Hidden Space of Ritual

*P*erhaps it was the long fast, perhaps it was the many days of darkness in the cave hidden away from what is seen, perhaps it was the constant silence. The boundary between this world and the spirit world began to blur. It was the time of my initiation. Out of the blackness came the voice of Guisso. "Malidoma, the time for remembering has come."

What did Guisso mean? Was he here or was it my imagination? Was it flesh or was it spirit? Is there any difference? I could not speak. It was not allowed. I wanted to reach out to my friend and mentor just to feel his presence, just to know that I was still alive.

"Guisso," my thoughts begged, "what is to be remembered?" My ears heard nothing, but his voice responded.

"Go back to the beginning, Malidoma. Go back even to the beginning of beginnings."

The beginning? The beginning . . . the beginning.

Yes. I can hear Grandfather's voice. All is warm and dark. The drumbeat of my mother's heart pounded with the steadiness of a trance dance.

"Little one, the time has come, while you are still in your cave of silence, to welcome you to the land of the living. The time has come to tell you what awaits you. A bumpy road awaits you, little one. But we are here to guide you on that road." It was the time of the fetal ritual hearing. People were gathered around mother, who was now in a trance. Her brothers and Grandfather were all there as well as the officiating *boburo* (the one who seeks the knowledge below) — shaman.

The voice of the shaman now was asking, "Speak to us child-who-is-to-come." Speak? How could I speak? Why speak? The warmth and the silence of the womb allowed me to remain tied to the Otherworld. To speak would be to touch the land of the living. Did I even want to do that?

"You must speak, you must answer my questions, child-who-is-to-come." The shaman's drum could now be heard. Its beat was growing louder than the drumbeat of my mother's heart. I was being lured, being pulled to the land of the living. The feelings, the energy of the living were rising within me, now too much to contain. I could be silent no longer.

"What is it you want to know?" I heard myself say. But it was the voice of my mother that was speaking this. It was the voice that talked to me before her sleep time. How could she be speaking the same words as I?

Grandfather's voice could be heard again. Even though he was a shaman-priest of great repute, it was customary to have a *boburo* officiate at the fetal ritual hearing. "I know that you shall come to us as a man-child. Tell us why you have been sent, your purpose for visiting us."

From the Otherworld could be seen the purpose. It was like a painting made of light that had no speakable form. The vision had no message made of words. To look at it was to feel its meaning. "I have come to walk with the enemy. I have come to wander in the house of the other, bringing the peace of water to the heat of yonder. I am to carry our name across the big sea. From the land of the *nipula* (white man) I shall carry the word of the Dagara. Gold shall flow with silver, East shall shake hands with West. To make an enemy a friend is to end the need for war, to vanquish the powers of destruction."

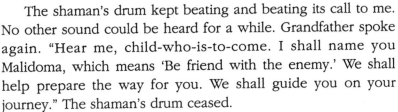

The shaman's drum kept beating and beating its call to me. No other sound could be heard for a while. Grandfather spoke again. "Hear me, child-who-is-to-come. I shall name you Malidoma, which means 'Be friend with the enemy.' We shall help prepare the way for you. We shall guide you on your journey." The shaman's drum ceased.

As the vision faded, the silence of the cave brought sounds that only silence brings. Where was Guisso? The voices of the ancestors seemed to chant, seemed to echo the approval of Grandfather's decision. It is the right of the grandfather to tell the grandson later what was said while in the womb. It is the right of the grandfather to give the name that will serve as a life program to its bearer.

Grandfather had always been my confidant and guide since the day I could walk. The first few years of a male child are usually spent with the grandfather while the other family members go on with their family responsibilities. There is an unspoken closeness between one who has freshly entered from the Otherworld and one who is close to returning to that Otherworld. Grandfathers want to know as much as possible about the state of affairs on the other side before returning. And the children will slowly grow into forgetting the grandness of the realm he came from.

Eventually, it is the role of the grandfather to direct the grandson to his father — thus creating a circle where a father (grandfather) allows a son (grandson) to be son to the father. Because of the intimacy between grandfather and grandson, the father tends to feel left out, and a kind of tension between the adult men develops. Until the grandfather dies or the child grows into adolescence, son and father do not have much of a learning exchange. The father does not have much to impart to the son because conversations between grandfathers and grandsons are like conversations of knowledge between brothers of a common group — that of the Otherworld. To know is to be old. Thus the father recognizes that he is presently too young to mess with this relationship between wise men — grandfather and grandson.

Initiation is the longest ritual one ever gets involved in within the village. In it there are things that can be talked about between initiates and things that can be revealed to non-initiates. But there are several specifics about certain rites or secrets that can never be disclosed. To do so is not just forbidden, it can be lethal to the discloser. One reason, is found in the sacred, hidden and silent space of ritual itself. It is there where things native to that space have no intention of being brought into the surface world so they don't lose their power or so they don't lose their ability to act the way they are expected or needed to act. It is like taking a fish out of water and expecting the fish to demonstrate its ability to swim. To prevent disclosure from occurring, the elders do something secretly to every initiate so that divulging these secrets will make the initiates dizzy, or suffocate, or go numb.

Language in itself does not create or provide a space in which the natural and the supernatural world can safely migrate into this world. Sometimes, the words into which we want to put certain sacred spirits are a deadly virus to those very spirits. So, rather than let themselves be damaged by us, these spirits damage us instead. I will have a greater opportunity to dwell on this topic of the danger of human language when I speak about initiation of the elders. For the elder who is usually officiating, hiding the nature of his relationship with a spiritual force is the way to keep this relationship alive. The relationship draws more strength, more power, and even gets more momentum within its hiddenness.

We call spirits into a circle of people in order to help achieve goals that cannot be achieved in any other way. This calling needs to remain in safe containment, the way a baby remains hidden prior to being born. Safe containment means keeping the space away from any impurities, any unwanted intrusions.

I still remember the funeral of my stepbrother that I talked about in the beginning of this book. Why was Grandfather insisting that everybody entering the ritual space be marked?

This helped save the ritual space from being a grooming place for more evil happenings. The marking was for security reasons but could have also been for reasons of secrecy, even though funerals are obviously a public rite. The implication is that what you see is not what you get. What was contained in this funeral was a secret mechanism destined to produce a counterforce against that which triggered the death of my stepbrother. It worked. For the traditional person, hiddenness is effectiveness. Hiddenness is power.

Disclosure or exhibition is threatening to the relationship between us and the spirits we invoke within ritual. Consequently, an outsider cannot be invited into a ritual already in progress unless that person is already in a ritual space of his own. This presupposes that every person you meet on the road has had a little ash and water ritual at home, and has spoken to his own ancestors before starting the day. This is common in the traditional Dagara world. No one can expect such a thing in the modern world. So when not sure, better to avoid taking risks. Intrusion into a ritual space is a profaning of that ritual space and the spirits invoked. The spirit will become agitated and will react as though the intruder intends to rip it open. Spirits care about your having called them in without telling them that there are intruders who intend to rip them open.

The profane is the allergy of the spirit. Within a ritual space, anything that is not sacred threatens to desecrate the hallowedness of what is happening. Consequently, it drives the spirit "crazy," and he who is in charge of the ritual is in big trouble. But when the space is kept clean, ritual yields great power to those involved with it.

Ritual as Show

The problem with Western culture is that it is a show-off culture that intimidates. This is why it is generating so much death, loss and displacement. To perform ritual for show is to generate some kind of death or loss. Concealment of ritual is an act of life preservation because it is only in its concealment that needs are met that cannot be met in any other way.

If our goal is to repair all the damage done by the powers of progress, it becomes important to make sure that we focus on how to stay underground while attempting to reconnect with true ritual and true spirits. People in the West are just beginning to retrieve ritual from the pits of their ancestral consciousness. Most of the time I see it coming out as fossilized debris that needs to be reinfused with life. Take, for example, grief ritual in America, which is performed at great cost using every decor imaginable. Such grief ritual induces the participants to focus on the pain of separation or digs out the repressed sorrow and sealed tears associated with the painful loss of loved ones. The focus here is not on ritual itself, but on opening up something in hearts and spirits that has been locked away so long that individuals can barely remember the source. I have witnessed funerals where wounded people in great need of healing (through ritual) are the ones actually planning and taking care of the funeral arrangements. These are people who need someone to help them in their own grief who are burdened with creating ritual space for themselves as well as others. We are facing here some kind of flawed process of self-caretaking. Who can create ritual in its proper space and sequence when there are no elders? Who is there who remembers the old ways, the ancient ways, the ways of the heart, the ways of the spirit that reach to the depths of the soul in its grief?

It is better not to do a ritual at all than to do one the wrong way. In the Dagara tribe, a failed ritual is repaired then and there because no one can stand to live with the damage of a ritual as it wrecks havoc on everything else in that person's surroundings. For example, with regard to the failed ritual I mentioned earlier, if we had postponed addressing the error immediately, it would have resulted in unfortunate physical damage that would have taken even more complicated ritual to repair.

It takes a ritual to repair a failed ritual. It also takes the person directly responsible for the failure to right the wrong. Acknowledgment of error is not error. A person who sincerely tells the spirit that he did something wrong cannot be punished anymore. The wrong itself is its own punishment.

Power on Display

As humans, we are fascinated by supernatural, spiritual power. Every moment you display this kind of power to the world, that power isolates you. You become displaced by the power you display because that power is also displaced through you.

For example, behind the mighty-looking corporations are a group of wealthy people whose personal lives are lived in marginality. To maintain the show of corporate power, they must give up something of themselves, their spirit. These people start to become invisible because they are mere instruments of the power being displayed, the power being made visible. They take a back seat to the corporation's need to be powerful. They then begin to lose touch with their own souls, with the world of the invisible. This is why they are marginal. The greatest needs ends up being expressed by these people and through these people.

It is the action of those in power that produces the poor, the menial worker, the man and woman in debt and the homeless. Misused power triggers its exact opposite as if that opposite needed to be there to highlight the dysfunctionality of its creator. The menial worker, the man and woman in debt, the poor and the homeless exist, as if they must, to highlight the person in power. The person who displays this kind of power needs more help than those who are, more or less, the casualties of this power display.

The power that is felt, entertained, nourished and kept alive from within through ritual has a much different effect on a person who may be a victim of overt power. This kind of power is what many people in the West seek avidly, and, in most cases, unsuccessfully. It is spiritual power, a power that is invisible, and yet whose presence can be felt in terms of gentleness, love and compassion. A person who lives in constant touch with the invisible realm of incomparable power is always in a good temperament and very understanding of people and situations. He does not fall prey to retaliatory invitations and does not experience wide swings in mood.

It is this kind of balance in a person that people in my village recognize as the presence of power in a person. This presence of power hides in a balanced person and speaks adequately enough about its aliveness. This hiddenness of power in a person is valued in my village because it speaks to life through its invisibility. This Presence of Power is not presence to the eye, but presence to the psyche.

Whatever happens in a ritual space, some kind of power is released if given a freedom in which to live. This is the only way those who participate in the ritual can continue to benefit from the power. The forces aroused in the ritual function like a power plant into which every individual is hooked. When one leaves the ritual space, the power of the ritual goes wherever the person goes. Only in ritual can the "here" follow you to the "there."

The more ritualized our space, the more ritualized our lives. I am suggesting that a space (cultural space or community space) in which ritual is the yardstick by which life is measured puts the people living in it in a constant state of ritual energy that sanctifies their lives. A sacred life is a ritualized life, that is, one that draws constantly from the realm of the spiritual to handle even the smallest situation.

Sabotaging Ritual Space

Once, on one of my trips back home, I came upon one of the men of the village wandering in the bush. He looked bewildered, his hair disheveled and his manner suspicious. Because I knew him and his family, I stopped to talk to him. His language was erratic and incongruous. To my greeting, he responded only with his eyes fixed off in the distant wilderness.

"The road that leads to town must be inside one of these trees. I've been searching for many seasons. Can't seem to see it. Do you?"

I was disoriented. I asked him what road he was talking about. "People think I have gone mad," he complained. "It is the whole world that has gone mad!" He began weeping and added, "How horrible to be the only sane person in a world gone mad."

I knew I could not continue talking with him. When back in the village, I asked what was wrong with him. A village acquaintance replied laughingly that he managed to steal the shrine of the ancestors with the intention of selling it to a group of white people. And he also spoke the unspeakable. "Where he is, is the place that his actions naturally put him." I realized that, to the village, this person was no longer alive, no longer existed. No one was either sad or happy about him. He was not there. In the meantime, the outcast thought that he alone was sane. The realization of what was going on in this man's world made me very sad.

It is important in ritual work to keep the content and purpose of the ritual space secret. Any attempt by any participant at disclosing the content of a ritual tears the group apart. To understand this, it is important to know that a ritual is a work of unification, or oneness with the gods and with each other. To disclose the ritual is to tear open a space that must remain hermetically sealed. Breaking this seal creates a decompression that affects everybody, including the person responsible. In the traditional world the person who violates the secret of a ritual becomes an outcast. The outcast is a person who has spoken the unspeakable or who shows the unshowable. What the outcast is doing is saying, "I no longer want to exist among you." When this happens, there is no cure for him, hence the final departure. I say there is no cure, but actually it is because the cure would require the rest of the group to suspend its current relationship with the spirit world and descend to the lower region where the outcast resides in order to rise up slowly with him. No one wants to do that, and so the outcast never gets reinstated, even when he wishes to. The concept of "all for one" does not work in initiation societies.

The principle of traditional groups is that its members are free individuals who entered the group freely. For a person to break the rule is not a sign of weakness or a momentary failure of the will. It is plain and irrevocable abdication or resignation from the group. A ritual must be done at this time to save the group from disintegrating as a result of this violent disconnection. To save an outcast, one must become an outcast. To become an outcast, one must lose one's power in the same fashion that the outcast lost his power. To lose power in that fashion means you never will have it back. Therefore to try to save the outcast is to become an outcast yourself.

The fundamental principle of ritual is that visibility threatens because visibility enslaves. When power comes out of its hiddenness, it shrinks the person that brought it into the open and turns that person into a servant. The only way that overt power can remain visible is by being fed, and he who knows how to make power visible ends up trapped into keeping that power visible.

What I am suggesting here is that power, as it is displayed here in the West, is extremely stressful to those who must work to display it. Western culture derives its power from machines or machinelike processes that are part of a Machine culture. This is a culture that gives names to corporations and treats

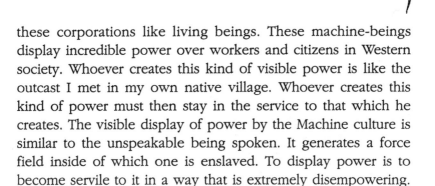

these corporations like living beings. These machine-beings display incredible power over workers and citizens in Western society. Whoever creates this kind of visible power is like the outcast I met in my own native village. Whoever creates this kind of power must then stay in the service to that which he creates. The visible display of power by the Machine culture is similar to the unspeakable being spoken. It generates a force field inside of which one is enslaved. To display power is to become servile to it in a way that is extremely disempowering. This is because the service is fueled by the terror of losing the fantasy of having power. ("It is the king who is ruled by the kingdom.") The man I met in the bush from my village was thinking that he alone was sane. In fact, he had the fantasy of sanity.

Those serving the culture don't have the option to slow down and address the issue of what to do with their own needs, or how to get in touch with their own unexpressed powers. For they are too caught up in the speed and motion that is required by the Machine to feed its overt power. But some ultimately become so distraught that they figure out a way to take care of themselves rather than to take care of something that can never be satisfied.

I am suggesting that the Machine culture, as described by David Kyle in his book, *Human Robots & Holy Mechanics,* is a violent break away from the realm of spirit just as the speaking of the unspeakable was a violent break away from those of us who held ritual space and the unspeakable realm of the spirit as sacred.

Ritual and Community

*G*randfather, why do you call me Brother Malidoma whenever you have something serious to say to me?"

There was a slight grin as he continued working with the herbs brought to him by my mother. He stored many herbs and medicines in his hut, which looked like an igloo made of mud. "You are the reincarnation of someone in the family who was very dear to me, my brother, Birifor. His is the name that is carried now by the entire family. So you are Birifor of the family Birifor. You were the elder son of my parents. You are my brother because, after the death of my brother, I was given the leadership of the family through the investiture ceremony. Your present father returned from the Gold Coast and took a wife, your mother. After your sister was born, I was told that my brother, Birifor, had been ordered to return to the family. It was an agreement between him and my father, Sabare, who was a great *boburo* (shaman-priest) and teacher of magic.

"A year later your mother was heavy with child. When the baby inside her would speak to me, he would begin by calling me brother. So you see, it was you who began calling me brother. I knew it was Birifor about to be born again, and I knew he would be a boy child. I waited until you came to life at dawn near the river between here and the white man's birthing place. I never wanted you to be born there. Besides, a man who is supposed to walk in a foreign land with foreign people must be birthed in the open air. Since then it has been my turn to call you brother. Now do you understand?"

"No, Grandfather, I don't understand." I was still only around five when this was told me. Grandfather knew that I would understand later. "I hear you call me Birifor. You do this as if you don't want to know that I am Malidoma. Why do you deny me my name? If I am Birifor, why do you call me Malidoma? And if I am Malidoma, why do Father and the others, like the priest on the hill, call me Patrice? How come I have so many names? Which is my true name: Malidoma, Brother or Patrice?"

"None of them is really your true name. But the one that comes the closest is the one that comes from the ancestors, the one that they address you by. It is Malidoma. Do you know why? Of .course you don't. So I am going to tell you why so it will look as though you asked me, OK?"

"Yes, Grandfather, tell me everything." I moved closer to him so I could catch every word and then hugged him.

"Patrice was bestowed on you by the white ones on the hill. Use it whenever you are in the world apart from the village. Brother is my name for you. Nobody else can use it but me. As for Birifor . . . well, no one is going to call you that. Malidoma is the name that you will begin hearing a lot when you become big, after you are initiated. So be ready to answer to it. You never know what name others will use. It is something that you will just have to learn to live with. That's enough for today."

Naming has always been an interesting power, no matter what culture you look at. It can be used to denote ownership, or friendship, or love or bigotry. It can be used in common for the sake of instilling community, or used in disparity to instill separation or preparation for war. And so I learned one more power from Grandfather — that my names and those that would use them would tell me at what level of community I would be interacting.

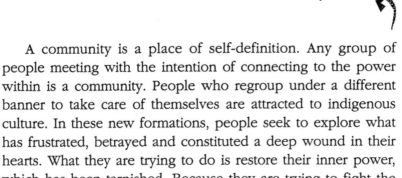

A community is a place of self-definition. Any group of people meeting with the intention of connecting to the power within is a community. People who regroup under a different banner to take care of themselves are attracted to indigenous culture. In these new formations, people seek to explore what has frustrated, betrayed and constituted a deep wound in their hearts. What they are trying to do is restore their inner power, which has been tarnished. Because they are trying to fight the servitude in which corporate power holds them prisoner, they are redefining themselves. They are moving themselves away from the magnetic visibility of externalized power. But to regroup against the Machine is to get out of control. However, one must not only be aware of this moving away, one must also be prepared to go all the way. To leave behind society and culture, one has to be prepared to do battle in order to be who you want to be.

Without a community you cannot be yourself. The community is where we draw the strength needed to effect changes inside of us. Community is formed each time more than one person meets for a purpose. Development of community depends on what the people involved consent to. What one acknowledges in the formation of the community is the possibility of doing together what is impossible to do alone. This acknowledgment is also an objection against the isolation of individuals and individualism by a society in service of the Machine. What we want is to create community that meets the intrinsic need of every individual. The individual can finally discover within the community something to relate to, because deep down inside each of us is a craving for an honoring of our individualism.

The first group of Americans I worked with showed me how much they needed to exist as a community. We drummed breathlessly for two days, prayed together to the spirits, walked together in the wilderness, did exactly that which village people do almost all the time to keep themselves together as a community. The intensity of the participants, their voracity in absorbing every lesson, was a learning experience for me. An African generally feels that Americans are content and satisfied with all the privileges bestowed on them by their society. This first group experience turned my thinking around the other way. What I sensed these people wanted was a certain means to relate to each other — a means that has nothing to do with what shopping centers afforded them. Above all, I learned that the most primitive instinct still lives in the midst of the greatest sophistication. Suddenly these people trusted each other enough to let go of their defenses. They trusted each other enough to want to be with each other in ways that no one taught them before. This is what I call the instinct of community.

A true community does not need a police force. The very presence of a law enforcement system in a community is an indication that something is not working. And the presence of the police is supposed to make it work. Such a force is essentially repressive, which means that certain people in such a dysfunctional community do not know how to fit in. A community is a place where there is consensus, not where there is a crooked-looking onlooker with a gun, creating an atmosphere of unrest.

In my village, houses do not have doors that can be locked. They have entrances. The absence of doors is not a sign of technological deprivation but an indication of the state of mind the community is in. The open door symbolizes the open mind and open heart. Thus a doorless home is home to anybody in the community. It translates the level at which the community operates. In addition, this community does not have a police force because it does not assume that the other person is dishonest or potentially evil. The trust factor must be high.

Elders say that the real police in the village is Spirit that sees everybody. To do wrong is to insult the spirit realm. Whoever does this is punished immediately by Spirit, as in the case of a newly wed girl who stole grain from the granary of her father-in-law. She sold the millet grains in the marketplace and then went into the bush to look for some dry wood to bring back on her way home. She found a dry tree and began to cut it down. It was not long before she cut herself deep in the arm. She arrived home bleeding and screaming. Her father-in-law rushed to the diviner. These kinds of accidents do not happen without a reason. The diviner revealed that his daughter-in-law was a thief who was purging her evil action. Because she transgressed the Spirit, she had invited an accident. The diviner added that the wound would not stop bleeding until she publicly admitted to the theft. It brought shame to both the father-in-law and the daughter. Her pleading guilty stopped the bleeding and allowed the wound to be dressed properly.

A functioning community does not need to peer at its members to make sure that they comply with the law. A functioning community is one that is its own protection. And one cannot form a community whose goal is to tear the rest of the society apart. A community that wants to "correct" the current sense of community is not going to survive.

A true community begins in the hearts of the people involved. It is not a place of distraction but a place of being. It is not a place where you reform, but a place you go home to. Finding a home is what people in community try and accomplish. In community it is possible to restore a supportive presence for one another, rather than distrust of one another or competitiveness with one another. The others in community are the reason that one feels the way one feels. The elder cannot be an elder if there is no community to make him an elder. The young boy cannot feel secure if there is no elder whose silent presence gives him hope in life. The adult cannot be who he is unless there is a strong sense of presence of the other people around. This interdependency is what I call supportive presence.

What is so good about being together with each other is that we can be the starting point for the possibility of building a larger community. Formation has to happen in a nurturing way if it is to work and prove itself to the rest of the world. In other words, it has to prove itself to be different, attractive and nurturing without the ambition of competing with the current dysfunctional communities supported by an army of policemen. And for this to happen, ritual must be the principal ingredient of its operating dynamics. Ritual must be constantly invoked as an opportunity for the weak to become strong and the strong to get even stronger.

The following is a partial list of the characteristics of a community, based on what I have observed in my own village:

1. **Unity of spirit**. The community feels an indivisible sense of unity. Each member is like a cell in a body. The group needs the individual, and vice versa.

2. **Trust**. Everyone is moved to trust everyone else by principle. There is no sense of discrimination or elitism. This trust assumes that everyone is innately well-intentioned.

3. **Openness**. People are open to each other unreservedly. This means that individual problems quickly become community problems. Being open to each other depends upon trust.

4. **Love and caring**. What you have is for everybody. There is a sense of sharing, which diminishes the sense of egotistic behavior. To have while the others don't is an expression of your making up a society of your own.

5. **Respect for the Elders**. They are the pillars and the collective memory of the community. They hold the wisdom that keeps the community together. They initiate the young ones, prescribe the rituals for various occasions and monitor the dynamics of the community.

6. **Respect for Nature**. Nature is the principal book out of which all wisdom is learned. It is the place where initiation happens. It is the place from where medicine comes. It nourishes the entire community.

7. **Cult of the Ancestors**. The ancestors are not dead. They live in the spirits in the community. They are reborn into

the trees, the mountains, the rivers and the stones to guide and inspire the community.

We need ritual because it is an expression of the fact that we recognize the difficulty of creating a different and special kind of community. A community that doesn't have a ritual cannot exist. A corporate community is not a community. It's a conglomeration of individuals in the service of an insatiable soulless entity. What we need is to be able to come together with a constantly increasing mindset of wanting to do the right thing, even though we know very well that we don't know how nor where to start. This seemingly frightening position is amusing to the spirit that watches over you. Your desire alone is strong enough to guide you along the path. But, of course, it is useful to know certain elemental steps such as invoking the Spirit of the Ancestors or of Nature. Knowing what spirit to invoke and what to do with that spirit depends on your ability to stay focused on your purpose. You must be willing to speak of your inabilities, your clumsiness. As Robert Bly would say, you must walk your limp in order to stay with your purpose. This is important for you to truly shine, to really be at home with yourself in ritual and in community.

Invocation is a call placed by a person to a spirit. To invoke the spirit is to call upon the invisible. The language of invocation must not be confused with order and command. It must be closer to a plea, a humble request. This is because ritual is a spirit-based activity performed by humans. For anything to happen, the ritual must be dominated by humility. We invoke spirits because we need their intervention in our affairs so that we can feel safe. Here is a typical invocation prior to a journey: "I greet you spirits of my ancestors; I greet you spirit guides, friends of the invisible. You that see without looking, you that know without learning, I come to tell you that I am about to go on a journey. How can a blind man travel? My feet can't hold me, my eyes can't show me the way, my wit can't guide me through traps. So I come to give myself away to you, that you may be my feet, my eyes and my wit;

that I may see through you, that I may walk with you, that I may feel you. For it is with you that this journey can happen as a journey. May it be safe."

This kind of invocation does not order the spirit to do something but requests that the spirit intervene in the process so that it might be good. It does not ask for assurance. It deliberately wants to trust that the sincerity of the words will yield the desired intervention.

Models of Ritual and
Constraints of the Modern World

*D*uring the months of July, August and September while mist still hung in the morning air, a different kind of "ritual" took place at Grandfather's door. A line of people would show up waiting to receive grain, usually millet, that Grandfather would give out freely. It was Grandfather's daily task to distribute food to all these needy people.

"Grandfather, why do these people have no food? Why do we have so much?" Grandfather graciously took a measure of millet from the woman whose job it was to measure the correct amount and proudly gave it to whoever was waiting next in line. He waited until the receiver was out of earshot.

"Brother Malidoma, we listen with the spirit realm. At night I look into my bowl of sky water [rainwater that has been collected before it ever touches the ground] while everyone else sleeps. If any animal harms or ravages our millet or nut crops I warn it away by shooting my upside-down arrow. If it persists, then I send another arrow to stop it from ever harming our crops again." I had heard about the secret of the upside-down arrow before. Grandfather was well known for having this power, especially during the war against the white man that was never won. He commanded great respect with this power.

As another person in need approached, I whispered, "Why don't these people shoot the upside-down arrow themselves?" The upside-down arrow was a kind of supernatural arrow that certain *boburo* (shaman-priests) could send to kill man or beast. It was kept secret except to those who were worthy of its knowledge.

Grandfather graciously extended another measure of millet. "Because they do not yet have ears that hear, nor eyes that see what cannot be seen and cannot be heard."

"Oh," I said rather matter-of-factly, not having the slightest idea what Grandfather meant.

At about noon when the sun was hot and Grandfather was tired of his duty, he would wake me.

"Brother Malidoma, my legs can't hold you any longer. Please allow them rest." I would wake up, half dazed with sleep and wonder what had happened.

The rite of charity being over, Grandfather would bring out food, and we would eat together. Grandfather was very frugal. Food was not to be taken unless one was hungry. If Grandfather saw any of the children eating unnecessarily he would bluster, "When you come of age, you will find initiation a bitter experience. Do not let the desires of physical satisfaction temper your warriorship. Remember, our ancestors are spirits. They feed their minds, and that is why they can do things beyond our comprehension."

Food was given a strange priority in the Birifor house. One ate only when absolutely necessary. Grandfather felt the same way about sleep. "Sleep is tribute too often paid to the body. The body is but a garment we give far too much attention to. Leave your body alone and it will align itself to the needs of the spirit that you are."

Frugality was a way of life around Grandfather. But others did not learn this lesson.

Our keeper of the Gate was known throughout Africa and parts of Europe as a man deeply connected with dimensional beings. People came from all over the world to meet him and to be healed by the spirits through the Gate he was in charge of. Europeans, whose needs were met, gave him lots of money. Error number one — he took it. Soon, he started charging them money for his services — error number two. In the end, only foreigners went to him. Village people, knowing that he had transgressed the law of the spirit world, would go somewhere else for their healing needs. Eventually, the spirit world abandoned him. He could not open the Gate anymore, nor could he effectively heal anyone. That was the end of his medicine-man career.

There are a lot of crooked people out there who sip the juice out of innocent people. One has to develop the smell that can detect the good from the crooked, the honest from the dishonest. For example, in the indigenous world where rapid changes are occurring nowadays, people have had to update their trust because money has intruded into everything, especially the spiritual. Would-be healers, and sometimes true healers, medicine men and shamans, have slipped away enveloped by the huge wave of money, making people aware that, in fact, they have lost their power to strangers who want to buy them off.

If indigenous people can tell the crooked from the honest person, it is because they live in the same community. In the West, people live in the illusion of a community and thus are unable to tell the difference between a real medicine man and a peddler. Their confusion is deepened by the intense craving for transcendence. Born and raised in a sort of isolation (no elders, no spiritual context in which to grow), they grow to become all needy, and so the first person that appears to have the kind of stuff they need is followed without reserve.

Modern cultures cannot, in their pursuit of the spirit, expect to reproduce the original indigenous way of existing. The modern world vibrates in such a way that it is impossible to translate or transplant. Anything aboriginal that enters the artificial space of Western culture is diminished, changed to fit into it. That which is indigenous can only live in a land that is indigenous. So in some ways, the shaman downtown is not the same as the *boburo* in the village because downtown does not emit the same energy as the village circle. But this does not mean that the modern-day healer is ineffective. It means that his status is commensurate with the situation in which he is supposed to work. And in this case everything he asks, as long as it is done with respect, honesty and integrity, cannot be looked at as a parody of spiritualism.

Money and Spirit

Can money and spirit be friends when ritual is involved? That is the critical question for indigenous people. It is my understanding that the pure sense of spiritual sharing should be devoid of financial intrusion. There is a kind of divinity in the dollar bill that is different from the divinity in traditional spirituality. The question I want to raise is whether these two opposing or competing divinities do influence each other as they become intertwined.

Opposites that meet certainly influence each other in ways that are sometimes catastrophic. And I know too, by experience, that opposites must follow each other because they need each other to maintain a proper balance. Consequently there cannot be a giver who does not receive. There cannot be a receiver who does not give. When we don't have these opposites paired, it voids the action because it lacks completion. I am talking about a kind of interchange that is equitable, that reminds both parties that something successfully happened and should serve as an example for others in the future.

In the indigenous world, when a diviner prescribes a ritual to be done in order to stop something from becoming bad, he expects you to come back with an expression of gratitude when everything is completed. This is not a payment for the work done. It is more like a symbol representing the circumstances that led to your interaction with this specific diviner. Later on, someone else encountering the same situation will come to the same diviner and the previous story will have been an illustration of what that other person is now going through.

Western culture is too comfortable with itself to change overnight. To think about changing this society is to evade the task we have toward helping ourselves as a people. It is more realistic to think about the spiritual needs of family and self as a starting point for social transformation than to begin thinking we can change Hollywood. The magnet of materialism is keeping people too busy to hear about spiritual change. In addition, the power of the Machine causes people not to hear what we have to say. The Machine is influencing a greater part of our lives than we think. To make Self each person's own best spiritual project is to avoid the crush of the gigantic modern Machine. Ritual enables us to live a life that is much closer to what our souls aspire to.

Industrial cultures live with the essence of two extremely dangerous phenomena. One is the good side of production; the other is the danger of what happens to the tools for production when they are devoid of any spiritual strength. Technology can and is supposed to be attentive to what liberates the person toward taking care of the higher level of existence. But, to me, the role of technology must be to attend to the lower part of human existence, since a thing devoid of the spiritual cannot help reach out to the spirit. The spirit liberates the person to work with the things of the soul. Because this reaching out to the spiritual is not happening, the Machine has overthrown the spirit and, as it sits in its place, is being worshipped as spiritual. This is simply an error of human judgment. Anyone who worships his own creation, something of his own making, is someone in a state of confusion.

Power and Corruption

In my own village I have seen medicine men speak things into disappearance or drastic transformation. I was still a little boy when I first saw it from my grandfather. It was one hot and sunny afternoon. We were both sitting under the only shade tree in the front yard of the compound. Grandfather was carving a hoe. A vulture that was sitting in the tree crapped on him. The bird's guano fell on Grandfather's bald head and splattered all over it, including his face. He spoke a funny vocalic language while trying to clean up the mess with his hand. The bird came crashing down and fell a few feet from us — dead. I leapt up to grab it. At the time, I did not know that we didn't eat buzzards. The bird was like ash. When I touched it, it disintegrated into some kind of porous substance. It felt as if there had never been a bird in that tree.

This power was bestowed upon my grandfather and others like him as part of their status as elders and healers, verified by their outstanding nature, their track record. Seeing this power, my young ego felt that if I were to possess such a skill I would almost worship it. But such power is not for worshipping, it is for reaffirming one's linkage with the divine. Industrial cultures are like a nursery of youthful exuberance too eager for immediacy of power. Consequently, powers are being acquired too fast, and as a result, those kinds of powers make victims of those who use them. The buzzard was killed because it did not honor the old. There is a point in indigenous life when the respect owed to a person does not just come from other people but from the natural world as well. Grandfather's status as an elder meant that he could order respect. He was in alignment with his title, which, as it was fouled, restored itself as the bird died. In addition, unlike children, who would take a buzzard shitting on them as a blessing or as a joke, an elder cannot because he has travelled the road that a child is yet to embark on.

In the village there is a strong censorship about the use of power because we know the dark side of a power that is acquired too soon. The gatekeeper, whom I mentioned earlier and who destroyed himself, got his power too soon. As a two-week-old infant he disappeared from the cradle while at the farm. People thought he had been eaten by a wild animal. They performed his funeral. But then the diviner said he was not dead. So they undid his funeral and waited.

Six years later, a child appeared at dusk accompanied by two-headed serpents, some wild goats with human heads and a variety of unrecognizable animal-looking entities. He said he belonged to a local family and that these followers were his friends. People vacated the family house in sheer panic. He sent his companions back to the mountain and settled in. People eventually came back to the house. From then on he began performing miracles just for the fun of it. Anything he saw and wanted, he duplicated it, or removed it from the hands of its owner.

I remember going into a local bar with him. He had money for one beer, so we spent it on a bottle of beer. I drank about six bottles' worth of that single beer. Each time the bottle was about to be empty, he would say a strange word, and it would become full again. In the meantime bottles of beer were disappearing in the refrigerator. This is what lead to his disempowerment.

Traditionally, one determines the accumulation of power that one needs. As one grows older in the village and demonstrates a character that matches one's age, more powers become available. Of course, there are moments when information is given to someone by error. The immediate consequence of such error is that the person gets crushed by it.

There was a guy who skipped initiation and who had promised someone in the national archive office that he would record what happened in the secret room of the elders' initiation. He recorded the initiation, at least part of it. What he heard destroyed him. He lost his mind, and a few days later was found hanging from a tree — dead. His crime was that he heard what he was not supposed to hear, and it stirred in him something that he could not contain.

What powers you possess put you at risk of becoming a victim of them. In the traditional concept, using the sacred for show will result in one being crushed by the sacred. The opposite side of the sacred is found in Western technology. One cannot live in harmony with technology; one serves it and is fed with the hollow hopes of being fulfilled by it some day. Christianity invented or blessed the invention of the technological Machine. The bulk of people in the Third World today have experienced Christianity not as separate from technology but almost as a part of it. Throngs of people went to school to learn to be modern — that is, to be Christian. Many ended up serving the administrative machinery of Christianity, hoping for a taste of greater modernism.

It was a team of Christians who came into my village over twelve years ago to ask those who went to church on Sunday to grow cotton so that they could buy it from them. The naive villagers saw in it an immense opportunity to become modern — that is, to acquire bicycles, short-wave radios and clothes. What they did not see was that these white Christians had their own separate agenda. Because they were in control, they laid out what they wanted the villagers to do. It included using fertilizer and pesticides that were banned in France. No one had the money, but everyone bought on credit. They were barely able to pay their debts out of their sales. With bitterness, the villagers returned to their traditional farming, but the land was angry. Tortured by foreign chemicals, it "went into a coma."

Technology was sent into Africa as an instrument of terror. Colonization could not have happened without it — followed by much destruction. I do not know why it feels to me that the Christianization of the Third World is fueled by guilt, but somehow the often violent zeal with which indigenous people were pulled away from their traditions, the lingering fear of sinning, going to hell, failing to pay dues, were all projections of a filthy Shadow.

The colonizers called this a "pacification mission." Then they came in to console those terrified by technology and converted them to Catholicism. My experience with Christianity in Africa is that its power does not come from Christ but from technology — and its corporate profile. Missionaries built churches, schools and industries and stirred a vibration, created a disharmony that displaced the indigenous person. Christianity is a technological Machine that ravaged and continues to ravage the indigenous world in Africa. The Church is unfortunately a part of it. It is the place where people are psychologically processed — even corporate people. And so I repeat, what powers you possess put you at risk of becoming a victim of them.

As part of the initiation rite, traditional people instill a secret homing device that prevents or guards against revealing or betraying sacred knowledge. A person becomes incapacitated each time he feels drawn by his ego toward sensationalism in repeating secret information about the sacred. For example, an initiate cannot say or do something that would produce a miraculous effect in front of people who have not participated in the kind of initiation that introduces people to these magical phenomena. So any person that feels the need to show power, and does so, is showing the end of his power at the same time. There are powers that, like a fish out of water, cannot function in the open air. In the village, the newly initiated person carries in himself something to prevent even inadvertent disclosure of sacred knowledge. This is what I call a homing device. It makes you feel like you're choking if you try to speak of this knowledge. And if you try to speak, it activates a certain suspension system within you causing you to choke. It is like an electric fence that restricts the space within which a domestic animal can roam.

A true African tribesperson cannot do whatever he or she wants abroad because distance does not hide him or her from the ancestors or elders. If I should make the error of disclosing something I shouldn't, the first time I return home and sit in front of an elder, he is going to begin by pointing to what I did, what I should not have done, and he will explain to me the damage that it does to me. The reason I am able to do it anyway is because what is within me has two functions. One is the function of a recorder that registers what wrongs I do so they might be righted at a cleansing ceremony. The other is prevention from making terminal errors. This one I haven't known because, and thank God, so far I have not done anything to provoke it. What is the value and the wisdom of having this protection device? It is a way to keep real power alive in the individual and in the community. Remember, the value of a ritual community is that it creates power that protects and helps all within the community.

My grandmother died in 1981. She was an extraordinary medicine woman, very secretive. If she were alive, she would kill me for telling my readers what she knew and did. When I see her, for instance, take on the body of a dog, because she's too old to walk to the farm, I imagine that in modern cultures this could be a great substitute for travelling by car and thus help eliminate pollution. I am not saying that everyone should turn into a dog to save the ozone layer. The dogs themselves might go on strike. But what I am suggesting is that there are powers available in which alignment between us and Mother Nature can produce wonder without messy side effects.

Licanthropy, transmogrification, the ability to take on an animal body, is not a science of externalization. It does not display or show off. My grandmother, as a dog, does not go around showing how effective she is, nor does she give any profane person the remotest opportunity to witness her transformation. The eyes of the profane have lethal effect on the transformation process.

Among the Mossi, the Dagara and the Dogon, taking the shape of an animal has several interesting purposes. One is healing. There is a medicine woman in a village close to mine who specializes in healing by transforming the person into the kind of animal in whose body the specific illness cannot survive. How she does it is her secret. That she does it is not illusion to anybody who sees it. In fact, no one is allowed to see it while it is happening. Everyone can see it after it occurs. Usually the transformed person goes, at first, into a fit of rage and panic. A pig might squeal incessantly until the human consciousness in the pig surrenders to the fact that what he is trying to say cannot be heard as words by humans. This is when the healing begins. Dogon and Mossi people transform themselves into animals for hunting purposes. Real animals can tell who is an animal and who is masquerading as one. But in the split second when they are trying to figure this out the hunter can shoot them.

From this I draw that Western technology is being put into the hands of people who have lost touch with the spiritual. Western Machine technology is the spirit of death made to look like life. It makes life seem easier, comfortable, cozy, but the price we pay includes the dehumanization of the self. To sleep in a cozy home, a good bed and eat great, chemically produced food you must rhyme your life with speed, rapid motion and time. The clock tells you everything and keeps you busy enough to forget that there could be another way of living your life. It has made the natural way of living look primitive, full of famine, disease, ignorance and poverty so that we can appreciate our enslavement to the Machine and, further, make those who are not enslaved by it feel sorry for themselves.

The Machine has made itself look beautiful by making other ways of life that have existed for tens of thousands of years look silly, shameful and uncivilized. But the truth is that the Machine must eliminate every alternative to itself and focus every attention on itself because it knows that its purpose is not to give life, but to suck the energy out of it. We have therefore come to the point where it is not possible to think of life outside of the context created by the Machine, from the traditional viewpoint.

I must say that progress is the invention of someone who suffered immaturity and who craved to be initiated. This could be the reason that nothing is definite, final, and yet everything is fast-moving. I still remember the first time I took one of my elders into the city of Ouagadougou and he beheld a multistoried building. The poor man was so shocked that he was speechless for a while. When he finally spoke, he said, "Whoever did this has some serious problems." Obviously the old man had never seen power displayed in public before.

Wherever there is technology, there is a general degeneration of the spiritual. This is because the Machine is the specter of the Spirit, and in such a state, it does not serve because it can't serve. It needs servants. It is like having an elephant in your home as a pet. Would the energy spent to find 200 pounds of food every day compensate for what you get out of it? Anyone whose genius is wrapped up in this kind of effort must devote his life to it.

The Structure of Ritual

*T*o be attracted to an ancient way of life is to initiate one's personal spiritual emancipation. No ritual can be repeated the same way twice (in my village there are seasonal rituals that are repeated — but never exactly). There are structures, however, that stay the same. Even in our drumming music we never have two people doing the same thing. I come into the drumming circle with my rhythm, with my talk. Somebody else creates a rhythm, and that person will then carry the rhythm. He has the burden to keep the rhythm going. What I do on the drum is my response to what I hear. So I talk back. I drum my feelings. That's my opinion. When somebody else comes in with another drumbeat, that is his own opinion. So, we end up with a whole brouhaha of opinions that an outsider might find extremely synchronic and rhythmical or chaotic and noisy. To drum is to hear.

This means that when someone cannot drum, that person has, among other things, a hearing problem. It is hard to create a rhythmical space with this kind of person. In the same way, it is hard to create a ritual space without calling the spirits. Invocation, as I mentioned earlier, is a call placed upon a spirit. When you invoke the spirit world you initiate a different context or condition by bringing in witnesses that are non-human. This is why the space in question is sacred. Sacred means where the spirit occurs. We can't make sacredness. The sacred is made by the spirits themselves. Here are some elements:

1. Invocational. Humans call on non-humans for a specific purpose. To meet as a group without invoking the spirits means that you are on your own.

2. Dialogical. We enter into a kind of solemn dialogue with the spirit and with ourselves. When we call in somebody who doesn't have a physical form, then we are giving a different contour to the place we are sharing with other people.

3. Repetitive. The actions (structures) in ritual are the same. When you pour a libation, the pouring stays the same.

4. Opening and closure. The ritual space is opened whenever the spirit is invoked. The ritual space is closed when the spirit is sent away. The spirit is sent away symbolically, not dismissed. And this happens when we tell the spirit that what we embarked upon is over and we are ready to resume normal life. We don't call people and then just leave them as if we had forgotten them. They will invent a way to remind us of their being there. Not closing a ritual space usually happens as an accident, or an incident, depending on how big the deal was in the opening of the ritual, and on what kind of spirit was called into the ritual space. Temperamental spirits such as the ancestors would likely trigger a major accident involving destruction. Nature spirits would rather cause a conflict. When they do, it takes a long time to get along with each other again. In ritual, *openings and closures are very important.* Whatever happens between these two extremes must be coming from the "pit of your belly," as village people say. This spirit structure is what is basic to indigenous ritual. At the end of a ritual the dimensional being who is called must be thanked and sent away.

A Ritual Sampler: The Funeral and the Language of Grief

*I*t was late in the afternoon when I first heard the sound. It was a shrieking guttural wail that shot out of several throats almost at the same time. It was echoed by other sounds in the near distance. The quiet of the village was lost in a matter of seconds. The voices were so sharp anyone would think they come from spirits lost in the human realm. I knew that something was wrong, but I could not tell what. A nearly three-year-old child wonders about everything associated with death. Grandfather would surely know about this. The last time this happened, it was because someone had seen something terrible.

"Grandfather, Grandfather," I called, breathless from my swift run to his hut. "There are spirits singing in the village. Something is going to happen. What is it?"

"Those are not spirits, Brother Malidoma. Those are the women of the village who are mourning your stepbrother's death. They are announcing to the rest of the village to prepare themselves for the grief ritual."

"How come you aren't making that sound, Grandfather?"

He smiled with a grin that betrayed his wisdom. "Only the women show such grief at this time. I must make ready for the ritual. And you must go, for I have much to do. The sacred space must be prepared. Your stepbrother must be sent to the place of the ancestors and we must help him. Now go with your questions. Your father will bring you to the sacred space later. You can watch and learn. I will answer your questions later. Go now."

I pretended to head back to my father's house, but instead hid behind a wall where I could see inside Grandfather's quarters. Whenever Grandfather had to be alone I knew something magical was about to happen. It wasn't very long before I saw him gather some of his things, among them the pouch that usually contained ashes. He quietly left, and I knew I had to follow. Grandfather has eyes in the back of his head. So I knew that he must be in deep thought not to see me following behind him. I tiptoed from house to house until I saw Grandfather arrive at what is called the ritual lodge. Other elders of the village were arriving also. They sat in a circle with Grandfather. Guisso, the special one Grandfather infrequently spoke of, also joined the circle. He was a little younger than Grandfather. They were quiet for a very long time.

I began to turn a beetle over with my toe, watching with childlike curiosity how it was able to right itself. After the third overturning my game was interrupted by a strange chant coming from the lodge. The elders had their arms raised up as if inviting guests in from the sky. With strained ears I could make out names of different spirits that they were asking to come and help. As the sound grew louder I grew more uneasy. The air around me felt alive, as if invisible fingers were gently coaxing me to go. And go I did. There was a time to be curious and a time to be smart. This was a time not to be too curious. I was to find out later that this was the beginning ceremony of the invocation of the spirits.

"Father, why is Grandfather in the ritual lodge?"

Father said nothing. He seemed caught up in thought himself. Or was it grief? He seemed upset with himself, as if he might be responsible for my stepbrother's death. How curious all of this was. The whole village was transforming before my very eyes. The wailing of the women could now be heard everywhere. It gave me goose bumps.

Several elders entered our house at that moment, saying not a word. Father grabbed me, pulling me out of the way. They marched like silent warriors. "Grandfather!" I called out. But not even his eyes moved. They all tromped into the room where my stepbrother had died. I wiggled, trying to get free, but Father would not let go. Straining to see the action in the sleeping room, I watched Grandfather throwing white ash into the air. The chanting continued. This time every word was loud and clear enough to start goose bumps again. Every conceivable good spirit was being called.

"One of the living just drew his last breath, his soul just left. Come, come to help us. Come, come to show my grandson the way to the realm of the ancestors." White ash was filling the air in the room. The chanting continued with its weaving and echoing of the sound of men. Outside, the wailing was coming closer, and the sound, all the sound began to flood the house of death.

I looked through the door to see Guisso slowly circling the house. He was carefully laying down ash, the same kind of ash that Grandfather had been throwing in the air. With only his eyes moving, Guisso gave me a curious look. I raised my hand in greeting. He said nothing, but I could see his lips pursing back a grin.

"Father, why are they putting ash around our house?" He bent down and whispered in my ear, "It is to keep any more evil from coming upon us. Vulture spirits sometimes are attracted to deaths like this and try to see if they can cause even more trouble." Vulture spirits? I had never seen one. I wanted to run to Guisso and ask him if he had ever seen a vulture spirit.

Emotion was taking the village hostage. Emotion was transforming even the air with its sound, its sights, ash and chant, wailing and waving of arms and the invoking of spirits. Never will I forget this first encounter with the mystery of grief.

A non-Westerner arriving in this country for the first time is struck by how little attention is given to human emotion in general. People appear to pride themselves for not showing how they feel about anything. A husband might lose his job yet deploy tremendous effort to show some modicum of indifference. A couple has a crisis in relationship, yet unless seen together, it is impossible to tell what turmoil they hide inside. And the worst case of all is witnessed when someone dies. It took me the longest time to figure out that a long line of cars with headlights on in the middle of the day meant someone had died. As attractive as the modern world is with its material abundance, it is repulsive with its spiritual and emotional poverty.

What overflows in the West is barren in the indigenous world, and vice versa. Among the things that the indigenous world can share from its abundance with the modern world are spirit and emotion.

There are countless ways of expressing emotion because countless ways are needed. No one is supposed to repress emotion. If death disturbs the living, it offers a unique opportunity to unleash one of the strongest emotional powers humans have: the power to grieve. Yet, anyone who has had an opportunity to participate in a grief ritual in another culture would be shocked by the effort deployed by people in this culture to prevent themselves from feeling anything when someone dies. It is as if death had intruded into forbidden territory of the heart trying to steal away with some kind of emotion against people's wills.

People die in newspapers, in television reports. People die on bulletin boards. But they are rarely shown dead. To an indigenous person, showing a picture of a person alive and saying that this person is dead is anachronistic. Why hide death?

People who do not know how to weep together are people who cannot laugh together. People who know not the power of shedding their tears together are like a time bomb, dangerous to themselves and to the world around them. The Dagara understand the expression of emotion as a process of self-rekindling or calming, which not only helps in handling death but also resets or repairs the feelings within the person. This is needed because death, and the sudden separation around it, puts the living in a state of emotional debt, loss and disorientation. The unresolved energy produced by the death of a loved one translates itself emotionally as grief. And grief is in fact owed to the dead as the only ingredient that can help complete the death process. Grief delivers to the dead that which they need to travel to the realm of the dead — a release of emotional energy that also provides a sense of completion or endedness, closure. This sense of closure is also needed by the griever who has to let go of the person who has died. We have to grieve. It is a duty like any other duty in life.

For the Dagara, grief is seen as food for the psyche. Just as the body needs food, the psyche needs grief to maintain its own healthy balance. As a result, one of the most sophisticated rituals designed by the Dagara for its own people is the funeral ritual. The Dagara feel this ritual, which involves everybody both living and dead, is owed to the dead, whether they die young or old. This ritual gives our people the opportunity to grieve individually and communally. I would like by way of example to express, to describe the process of this communal expression of grief as it is experienced among the Dagara of Burkina Faso. I would also like to describe grief and its expression within a ritual context.

Grief is an aspect of the Dagara social life. And death is where it is chiefly expressed. Death is not seen as an ending but rather as an opportunity for a person to take off these ragged clothes we call a body, and walk naked. Even though this is a view commonly held by the Dagara, death still produces a kind of sudden vacuum and loss of attachment that requires grief in order to heal. Without grief, the separation between the living and the dead never actually shifts into that stage in which the living accept the fact that a loved one has become a spirit. The departed loved one consequently never arrives where death commands him or her to go and, therefore, becomes angry with the living.

If there is no expression of grief, it will affect the dead and the living detrimentally. The dead cannot then go free from their earthly consciousness. As the deceased takes on spirit essence, he or she may get snagged into thinking of himself or herself still as a person. Thus, the deceased may begin to intrude into the business of the living in a way that can constitute a serious nuisance.

I remember once looking for an apartment in town where I was a student. The rental-office lady took me to a nice-looking efficiency apartment on the second floor of a building. As soon as we entered the place, I was frozen by a dismal sight. There at the kitchen sink stood a girl in her twenties with a kitchen knife two-thirds into her chest. She was bleeding profusely with her white robe soaked in blood down to her feet. It took me a second to realize that she was the ghost of a person who had been dead for quite a while. My reaction startled the housing person who was showing me the place. Of course she saw nothing. She asked if there was something I did not like about the place. I said yes. She asked what. I could not tell her what I saw. I said it was a vague feeling that I should look somewhere else. This is what happens when a dead person is not grieved. It takes a living person to shed tears on behalf of a dead person for this kind of thing not to happen. Humans must feel grief and be able to express it sincerely in order to free the dead spirit.

In the village there is an opportunity to grieve daily because there is death almost every day. And funeral rituals last long enough to produce a continual opportunity for the expression of grief. It takes a great deal of involvement within a community for grief to be expressed freely. It is the presence of the community that validates the expression of grief. This means that a singular expression of grief is an incomplete expression of grief. A communal expression of grief has the power to send the deceased to the realm of the ancestors and to heal the hurt produced in the psyches of the living by the death of a loved one.

The ghost I saw in that apartment was perhaps grieved for only a few hours, maybe less, and by a few people only. Those who came to support the family in grief were probably trying their best to make sure that the members of the family did not shed too many tears. They were preventing grief from happening rather than encouraging it. They themselves were without tears, and so the poor deceased girl never went away. Tears carry the dead home. Communal grief therefore provides the opportunity to reach that important cathartic peak that grief must logically lead to, as well as serve as an energy that transports the dead home.

Grief is an energy that works at mellowing the mind, heart and body. An agitated or prolonged expression of grief exhausts the body to the point where rest is needed. One notices that a baby sometimes cries heavily before going to sleep. Grief takes us to the top of the hill and then lets us walk back down slowly, peacefully. It helps relieve the person who is in sorrow and leads him or her toward acceptance of the phenomenon of death, separation and love.

Funeral rites in a Dagara village usually start shortly after the death. The first people to cry out loud are the women. By wailing, they are not ritually involved, but are merely sending the news to the nearby villages about what has happened. While women are wailing, men are performing the invocational ritual that will make it possible for the funeral to proceed out into the open air for the next two or three days — depending on who dies. To hear women cry means that someone just died. The reason that men don't cry is because they must create the ritual space for the funeral to begin. Their ritual sets the space for the communal expression of grief. The elders gather in the ritual lodge to tell the ancestors that one of the living just departed, that he will soon be on his way to their ancestral realm and that the villagers will need all their help to make that happen.

Every conceivable good spirit must be evoked to make certain that the deceased properly journey to the realm of the ancestors. No one wants to be responsible for having the deceased not reach the realm of the dead. For the responsible person may die to join with the one who cannot find his way.

Twelve years ago, I lost one of my best friends this way. His departed father, who had died in his hands but a few weeks earlier, had come back to get my friend because his mother would not allow the rite of the dead to be performed. She was Catholic. The priest had told her the rite was Satanism. Her son died suddenly in the city, hit by a car that disappeared before anyone could read the license plate. Back in the village, the diviner found out that the father of the newly deceased son had been sitting at the gate of the realm of the ancestors for a long time, waiting for the final ritual that would have thrown the gate open. In total despair, he had come seeking the most spectacular way to alert the family to the difficulty he was facing. A spirit who cannot find his way to the realm of the dead is dangerous to the living.

Invocation and the Funeral Ritual

The invocation itself looks very simple, involving the throwing of white ash by a priest called the ash thrower. The house where the death occurred is circled with a ring of that ash to prevent evil spirits from penetrating the room where the invocation is taking place. Like vultures, evil spirits are usually attracted to a ritual such as this. The spirits are invoked mainly so that they can come to help the deceased in the journey ahead by squeezing enough emotion out of the hearts of the grievers.

There are three elements in the funeral ritual that are in constant interaction: the musicians, the mourners and containers, and the assembled villagers. This interaction is needed to maintain the power and the energy that steers the grieving. The music group consists typically of two large xylophones, one single drummer and two singers. These singers are improvisers whose function is to recreate and reproduce, through their singing, the history of the family up to the death that resulted in the separation. The singing theme combines the deeds and the sorrows of the family. Words stir the grief when they concentrate on the absurdity of the cycle of life and death with love in between. But words carried by music have an even greater impact on the display of grief. The xylophones weep the tune, the drum dramatizes the circumstances, and the singers verbalize the event. Everybody else then becomes free to express his or her own emotional response whichever way it comes to him or her. I call these singers cantors because their chants are worded spontaneously around the life of the person who died, in order to focus and steer the communal grief.

The dead person is seated a few yards away from the weeping crowd on a wooden stool freshly built from a special tree. The same tree is used to build a shrine around the dead. The dead person is dressed up in full ceremonial regalia. The shrine is decorated with colorful fabrics and with the sacred objects that belonged to the person now dead. The shrine represents the place from where the dead reaches out to the great beyond. Two women elders are consecrated to take care of the corpse. They each sit on one side of the corpse with fresh leaves in their hands representing the new life that has started for the dead person. They also use these leaves to chase flies away from the dead body. These women elders, although they weep discreetly, must be inattentive to what is happening outside the space in which they sit. This is because they are accompanying the dead person, collecting all the grief poured into the space and loading it on the soul of the dead one as it readies itself for the grand departure.

Between the shrine and the people there is an empty space thatrepresents turmoil. It is the place of chaos and turbulence. It is the place where disorder must be acted out. It is the sacred space. In it every form of emotion is permitted, encouraged and expected. People are free to get angry and to shout out loud to God and to any spirit. People are free to make any absurd comment they have as long as it pertains to the phenomenon of death and translates how they feel about it all. They can dance their emotions, run around in response to a strong urge or just weep their guts out.

Behind the singers and the musicians stands the crowd of people who have come to join in the ritual after hearing the initial wailing of the women. In fact, every person in the village is obligated to join in the expression of grief that follows death. Any stranger who happens to pass by the ritual space during the grieving must also stop, pay respect and either join in or walk to the place where the deceased is seated. There he can pay respect before continuing on with his business. This means that death stops every activity pertaining to life and disrupts the continuity of human feeling and relationship.

Death is chaos visiting the quiet of human life. Consequently, it is criminal to pursue business as usual knowing that someone in the village has died. Such behavior would indicate that one is used to death — which is impossible. For no one can get used to the idea of death, and to villagers, no one is supposed to get used to it. Not to participate in the ritual means one is evading what one owes the dead (and this is criminal since it traps the dead between here and beyond). Not to participate can also pollute one's life because the living cannot live peacefully until the dead are really dead, gone to the realm of the ancestors. Death requires the suspension of normal activities.

The people who gather for the funeral ritual are grouped in specific ways. On one side of the musicians are the male villagers, the female villagers on the other. These two groups constitute a formation capable of functioning rhythmically and harmoniously with the actions of the instrumentalists and singers. Within these gendered groups are two other groups, consisting of the mourners and the containers. The mourners grieve. The containers make sure the mourners do not go beyond the ritual space nor do anything that is harmful to themselves or to the villagers as a whole. Mourners are usually close relatives of the deceased. They feel the separation more acutely than the rest of the village. Their feelings, a combination of the desire to join their loved one in the great beyond and a deep frustration with life's vicissitudes, make them prone to a lot of violent displays. They are insane in a way.

Keeping their insanity bearable requires a trail of people who are not as upset as the mourners. These containers typically are relatives who come from afar. Next to them are those who are just villagers, friends or friends of friends. They are there to keep the sacred space alive, to contain the chaos within it by assisting the mourners. Thus, the whole village attends the funeral in order to help the family and relatives express their grief. The villagers also take this opportunity to bring their own unfinished business with their own dead relatives. In the largest sense, the ritual is not only about this one dead person but a ritualized process that encompasses all the dead of the village up until then.

One can recognize those arriving at the funeral ritual for the first time by their check-in ceremony. Any person who enters the ritual space must first walk three times past the dead in a straight line. At the fourth passing the newcomer must walk toward the dead twice and make an offering as a presentation from himself and his own dead relatives and parents before joining the gathering. Offerings, or give-aways, are usually in the form of cowry shells or domestic animals. Cowry shell offerings are thrown into the shrine circle because no one can enter it except the two women elders in charge of the body. Participants throw in anything of substance or otherwise that will help the soul go away on its journey to the Great Beyond. Other offerings are directly presented to the primary mourners through an intermediary. The intermediary must be a distant relative.

Everyone must do the check-in ceremony. This is why people notice when you don't go to a funeral ritual. Sooner or later a death will occur in your own family, and you'll find that the relatives of those people at whose funeral you didn't go will hesitate before they come to yours. If they come, they come to make a statement about your declining sense of community, and they will do that in a singing fashion. In their song they will describe how the person was not at their relative's funeral. They will emotionally harangue you on social ethics pertaining to death and the responsibility that weighs on everybody who learns about the death of anybody. Consequently, a person's social failures are brought out in the course of funeral ritual, and as a result create an occasion for a special kind of grief. Death reminds the person who is not paying his or her social dues to the community that he or she must repent and grieve for past failures.

In the funeral ritual, the xylophones are always the instruments that set the primary melodic influence. Their role is to produce a musical space so that the wailing that accompanies grief can happen in melody. They are divided into what we call the male xylophone and female xylophone. The male xylophone follows the mood of the singers while the female xylophone accompanies the male xylophone by creating a set of notes repeated over and over. After a while the drummer enters, creating a rhythmical space within which this chanted verbal dialogue can happen. When the male singers enter they lead the rest of the group into a chanting expression of grief. Cantors speak to each other as if no one else is there. One cantor will come forth, with a very incisive statement about humans being trapped in a world in which they are not in control because of the mighty power of death. They will go on to sing that the family whose relative has died has been chosen in order to have everyone remember that our death may be next. Another cantor will respond very quickly with a short sentence sung at a high pitch, and as he sings, all the men will initiate a chanting pattern that will then be taken up by the group of women, finally involving the whole group of family members, relatives and villagers. Meanwhile, the cantors continue to speak to each other about death and the dead. The pattern is repeated endlessly, and the dialogue between the cantors is extremely diversified.

In between the cantors' dialogue there are individual or sub-group expressions of grief. While the group is involved in chanting its sorrow, individuals may get in touch with areas inside of themselves that require specific grief attention. These are moments when individuals separate from one of the groups and allow themselves to be carried away by the energy surging in them. People feeling this deep grief wail in the direction of the shrine and within the space of chaos in an attitude of despair. As they near the shrine, the sacred place representing the great beyond, other people (usually containers who had been walking discretely behind) will touch them on the shoulder. The touch is a reminder that they must throw their grief into the sacred space of the shrine and return to the village to gather more grief. They must not walk into the sacred space of the shrine, for this would mean their death. To walk into the sacred space of the dead without being consecrated is to join with the soul of the dead as it gathers the fuel of grief to march into eternity. This is why mourners should never be left alone in expressing their grief. The vulnerable state of a mourner predicates him or her to sudden death, grief being an expression of the pull toward death and eternity. My father lost his first wife this way. As the funeral of her daughter was progressing, the poor woman had a "grief seizure." She ran wildly toward the shrine. A female container on her heels touched her as they both neared the sacred space. She ignored it and leapt into the space. People were bewildered by the sight of her in a place like that. But nothing happened until the next morning when she did not wake up. By noon, the bodies of a daughter and a mother were sitting together in the same sacred space.

The more one grieves, the more one gives to the dead and the more one moves closer to being with the dead. The container's task is to ensure that the mourner knows well how to distinguish between a grief that helps the dead soul go home and a grief that kills. Such a person is never left alone. The container is a caretaker who comes out of the crowd to join in support of the grief-stricken person. He or she operates as a space provider on the one hand and, on the other, as a lifesaver who brings back home someone who would otherwise mourn himself or herself into eternity. Such a person will duplicate every action channeling grief that the mourner expresses and will do so almost synchronously, but while doing this, he will keep a keen eye on the other who may go out of bounds anytime. Containers do not trust mourners. It is assumed that any individual expression of grief increases the danger of breaking the ritual space. Consequently the assistance from a person who does not feel the urge to express his grief in this particular way is like having the extra eye that knows where the boundaries are.

Among the participants, the members of the immediate family of the dead are tagged with a rope on their wrists for identification purposes. These are called *kotuosob*, which means the-center-of-the-heat people or primary mourners. These people are at a high risk of grieving themselves to death and are therefore more likely to go out of bounds and break the pattern and order of the ritual. They are tagged for everybody to recognize. The more intensely the cantors sing in reference to them, the wilder their expression of grief. There are people assigned to look after these tagged ones for the duration of the ritual. These caretakers will mimic exactly what the tagged relatives do. For example, if a relative begins to run off, they will follow until a certain point at which it becomes necessary to remind the relative that he or she is moving out of the ritual space. Most of the time relatives get so caught up in the grief that they will dash out of the group and run wildly in any direction. The caretakers have to keep pace with them. Caretakers are always at least two feet behind these grievers, and do exactly what they do. Most of the time these actions end in the form of a rhythmical dance that consists of pounding the ground with the feet and in jumping up and down in cadence of the drum.

Non-relatives who are not tagged with a *kotuosob* express their individual feelings in a less risky way. It is assumed that in the grief ritual space all will be moved to express themselves. Sometimes, a large group of fifteen to twenty people will come out to join a primary relative battling with his sorrow. The whole group will end up as a line of dancers dancing exactly what the relative is doing in the front of the line. It is understood in the ritual that the feeling of the person in front of the line will be transmitted to every person as they dance together in one line.

This sharing of personal feeling is a form of silent and physical support to the person grieving. The dancers will move back into the surrounding groups when the person in the front stops dancing, turns around and starts walking toward the chanting crowd. At that moment, one after the other, the dancers will do as the grieving relative does.

Within a grief ritual space, expression of grief is gender-specific. No woman will try to assist a man in grief, and no man will help a woman to express her grief. It takes a man to provide an outlet to the emotions of another man. Similarly, it takes a woman to echo the grief of another woman. But while all that is happening, the drummers are drumming, the xylophones are playing, the singers are singing and even those dancing continue to partake in the communal chanting. And this goes on for at least three days and three nights if the departed one is an adult. Children's funerals last one day. Adolescents' funerals last two days and one night.

There is yet another category of people whose role it is to downplay the emotional intensity of the relatives' grief. In contrast to those who assist the members of the primary family stirring their grief, this other group acts out the whole ritual as if it were a joke. They call this group *laluoro,* or the joking partners. Their function is to act like a thermostat. They keep the inner space of the ritual under control because the Dagara believe that grief can kill when it is carried up beyond a human level of intensity. These joking partners are needed to balance the energy of grief to an appropriate human level. Joking partners will always leap at a primary member who goes wild and will ask for cowrie shells, for instance, or remind the person of the fact that he brings food to someone (the dead) in the compound who is not hungry. They can also be seen at the shrine talking to the body of the dead. It is not surprising to hear them say to the dead, "Now let me see you do as you used to do if you're a real man," or "I've always asked you to be quiet, and you have never listened. Now you are still and quiet without my asking, and I am the one making all the noise. How about that?"

Although these reminders appear to have no connection with what is going on, they are very effective in grounding an individual at the extreme end of expressing grief. No one escapes the emotional energy triggered by such a ritual. Everybody gets the opportunity to shed some tears, and regardless of the purpose for which the tears are shed, the dead will have plenty of tears to swim in on the way home to the other world. Of course, the burial ceremony itself is not as important as the expression of grief because burial occurs after the general grief catharsis has been achieved. If this catharsis does not occur properly, the spirit of the dead will not be able to leave the village and, in time, will have to kill more people in order to have companions to be with around the village. Or the funeral of the latter will collect enough tears to carry both to the other world. What is certain is that a village in turmoil is a village that has some unfinished business with its dead. Any premature death is caused by an imbalance of energy between the living and the dead. This is why, when death occurs, the thing to think about is not burial, but funeral, tears, grief.

The Re-enactment

Besides the xylophone, drumming and singing to stimulate the grief catharsis, there is another important part to the funeral ritual. The life of an adult who dies must be reenacted by the surviving members of his initiation group. All the males who were initiated at the same time as the departed one will, in the second or the third day, re-enact that person's life. That portion of the ritual is called *xanu*. It means dream, as if the dead were dreaming his life. The spirit of the dead must live its life once more in an accelerated fashion before departing to the realm of the ancestors. A number of token activities about the person such as farming, weaving, carving, hunting, drinking or divining are quickly acted out by his friends. In a way, this is a ritual of their separation from the dead. It is believed that doing what was once done frees the living from the dead and vice versa, thus allowing the dead to reach the realm of the ancestors. Going to the ancestors is also getting the permission to come back eventually. But it is important for the dead that the living do what they are supposed to do to allow the dead to be able to come back. In a community, the death of one person is the affair of everybody. Therefore, it takes everybody to send the dead to the realm of the ancestors. Any isolated, individual effort to perform ritual that requires community effort will only result in having the departed one come back as a ghost. The ghost will try to tell the family what must be done for the dead person to get the chance to register with the ancestors. This in turn makes it possible for the person to return to this life at a later time.

This re-enactment of the life of the deceased is done in the following manner. Individuals who have a personal relationship with the dead are chosen to represent the deceased. This role of representation will shift from person to person because no one can play the role of his dead friend for a long time without going crazy. Changing roles prevents one from staying in it long enough to reach this apex of feeling.

Speeches and the Pyre

There is yet another aspect of the funeral, one that regroups the participants around the funeral pyre and takes the form of speeches. The friends of the deceased express their friendship one last time. Each person narrates the genesis of his friendship with the deceased and makes an offering to the dead to take along with him on his journey to the realm of the ancestors. An immediate relative of the deceased accepts the offering so as to continue the life of friendship and love that the giver had with the deceased person. Acceptance of the present is an acknowledgment of the transfer of relationship. Friends who had a strong relationship with the deceased now have this same relationship with the person to whom they gave the present. Through this ritual of transfer, the dead one never really goes away because it is through this person that his invisibility is transcended. The living person who accepts the present is now in fact the dead person for everyone in the village. The sincerity with which the villagers then interact with the person will attest to that role.

In the case of the death of one's parents, the surviving children are not concerned with this transfer ritual. You don't replace a mother or a father because you never lose your father or your mother. The sisters of your mother will be hurt if at your mother's death something happens that suggests replacement. The same is true with the brothers of your father. What is important in ritual transfer is that it concerns itself solely with friendship ties born out of shared experiences such as initiation, hunting, farming and the like. The ritual transfer of friendship therefore concerns those who feel they must continue the friendly tie with someone in the family of their deceased friend. Elders say nothing can destroy a true relationship, not even death. To grieve a dead friend does not erase the friendship with him or her. Such an attachment can become dangerous if left without an outlet, that is, if it is not transferred on to a living person. When love exists, it must continue, or it will turn dangerous for the person who loves. Human feelings are an energy that can turn dangerous, negative, if not honored. So when a loved one dies, those who survive must reconnect the "plugs" from the dead person to people who are still alive. They do that partly because of the sense of loss that any death produces and partly out of the desire to give a certain continuity to emotional relationships.

Every person, male or female, who dies a normal death is given a full range of funeral ceremonies. If the dead are not given these ceremonies the dead are stranded between worlds. An unweaned baby who dies does not get this kind of ceremony. An uninitiated person gets to be mourned but does not benefit from these internal rituals because he is an outcast with respect to his age group. Consequently, to evade initiation is to deny yourself a proper death.

Modernity and Death

With the sweeping transformations changing indigenous way of life, elders are more concerned about dying properly and having proper funerals than ever before. They want to be sure they will have a normal funeral ritual performed on their behalf. But they also interpret people's refusal to get initiated as the first sign that death is being evaded. Being seduced by Western modernity, villages are being told initiations and funeral ceremonies are both wrong and unimportant, that they are uncivilized and primitive. This is because modernity sees death as an end while the traditional world sees death as a transition.

Some conservative families in the villages try to figure out alternative ways of taking care of this problem by asking each other to be responsible for the initiation of their children. The first consequence of westernization has been to make initiation private. In the old days, initiation was a village matter that mobilized the energies of every person. Today, a negligible energy is invested in it, and it is done by those who still cling desperately to tradition. These people still believe that a person cannot mature without initiation. Anatomic maturation is insufficient for manhood or womanhood. The experience of breaking down fundamental perceptions of the world brought about by the initiation ritual permits another self to grow and to be born. Without this other birth, there can be no meaningful death.

Initiation and death are linked together in an intimate way. There is some sense in which one can say that death ends the initiation process. But this ending must be accomplished by the living in the form of an energy released through ritual grief. The loss of initiation in the traditional culture opens a psychic spiritual hole that is rapidly destroying the soul of my people. It shows that when the modern and the traditional collide something happens that inevitably sets the deterioration of the traditional into motion. The indigenous purity of life is also its vulnerability. When touched by something less than pure, it takes on the impurity of the other and loses its identity in the process. Likewise, the loss of initiation also inspires the loss of one's ability to grieve regularly in a community context and creates a condition that traps the person in a meaningless and wayward life pattern.

In conclusion, the components for the maintenance of grief energy begin with the ritual done by the elders at the Nature Shrine shortly after death has occurred. Ash throwing, the ritual that opens the space for the funeral ceremony, is designed to avail a working space devoid of any perturbing forces so that the throwing of oneself into grief can be strong enough to propel the dead to the realm of the ancestors, where life continues. This ritual opens the space within which grief can be expressed in a productive and practical manner. When death occurs, no male utters the sound of grief until a ritual space is created. Because funeral ceremonies enable the dead to begin life with the ancestors, grief is the major process for release from this life and movement into the next.

Women can wail so as to signal people in the nearby compounds that a grief ritual is about to start. But they cannot participate in ritual grieving until they've heard a male voice. There is a specific way in which the male announces the news by using his voice. What the male voice says in a condensed way is "Yes, we have a death, but also the ritual space has been created. We can now mourn. We can now grieve."

The second part is actually the musical space constructed by a xylophone, a drummer and a couple of singers. There is a close relationship between music and grief, and so, when the space is created, music must go on all the time for grief to express itself. So the musical space is an important part of the maintenance of this force field that is created. It permits people to grieve.

The third part is the contained expression of grief and the re-enactment of the life of the dead person. The people who normally take care of this are self-selected. They are people recognizable by their ability to act. They are called the communicators or the mineral people. They act (whenever they are among a group), tell stories, recite genealogies and know nearly everything that has happened in the village. But to be in the funeral they must be people from the same initiation group as the dead one. The final parting ceremony takes place around the body of the dead, which is sat up and dressed in special ceremonial attire. This is the last ritual time to express unformulated grief. It's usually the most powerful moment because this is where the physical separation happens and people have to let go, usually holding back some of their grief until that time when they finally realize that they have to let go. While they grieve, the gravediggers come and take the corpse away. Nobody follows the gravediggers to the burial site in the cemetery.

The dead are laid sideways on the grave facing east (west for men), next to items that are important for their journey. These items could be a medicine pouch, a divination item or the whole medicine bag if it is determined that this is what the spirit of the dead wants in its journey to the realm of the ancestors. This must be done right, or the dead will not let the burier — who must descend into the grave to arrange all these things into proper order — leave the grave.

The act of burying a person is a sophisticated process that requires people who are trained to do it and who possess this particular kind of medicine or knowledge.

The grave is shaped like an egg, with a tiny opening in the middle big enough for the body to go through. It usually takes two people to put the person in the grave. There is one person inside the grave to receive the body and to lay it the right way, and another outside the grave who hands the body in and who must stay to assist the person working inside the grave. The task of proper burial is basically the responsibility of the person inside the grave. This person must lay the body in its ritual posture with the clothes and the accompanying items properly arranged. If he does it right, he will leave the grave without being touched by the body. If something is not done exactly right, he will know it when he begins to exit the grave because the spirit of the dead will use the hands of the body to grab the legs of the exiting person. If this happens, he will then have to get back into the grave and redo everything he did before and try another exit.

Sometimes it happens that the dead will play a game with the person inside the grave. Although this is very rare, it usually happens with witches and powerful medicine men who, for one reason or another, always find something wrong in the way they are being laid in the grave or in the way their things are arranged. It takes a witch to bury a witch. When everything has been done properly, the inside burier uses magic to escape. The person waiting outside closes the exit of the grave and heads back to the village, where he will find his companion who used magic to escape waiting for him.

Using magic is the only way one can escape when the dead one doesn't want the burier to go. So there is a kind of magical element in the disposal of the body that is not explicable, because it belongs to the secret society of those who bury people. Children are allowed to take a look at the grave before they bring the dead into it because the children are the symbol of the possibility that the dead will be remembered. The physical structure of graves is such that they blend into the natural surroundings after a few years. But not everybody is buried in nature. Elders are usually buried in the middle of the family compound. Their graves are shrines where all kinds of rituals are performed. An elder, being a person who has completed his mission here on earth, is expected to spend a lot of time as a counselor helping the living from the other side. For a while he or she will appear in leaders' dreams in his or her earthly body. But after a long time has passed, the leader, as an ancestor, chooses to appear in visions as an animal or a tree. Ancestors often cast off the idea of appearing to the living as humans. They return to nature and to forms of earthly configurations such as mountains, rocks and rivers. The spirit of the elder is family-centered and very specific in the kind of direction he wants the family to follow. This is why elders are not buried in nature but at home. It is the highest honor given to a person in the village. To be buried in the family compound is the reason everybody looks forward to being an elder.

The Farewell

*T*he stirring of the baobab tree called me from my sleep. Even though it was not close by, it sounded as if it were. There seemed to be a strange ether in the air. Even though I was only five years old, I knew that something was amiss. Something was different. As I sleepily sauntered from Father's house, I noticed Guisso sitting close to the door. He spoke to me. "This will be a special day, Malidoma." Guisso never spoke to me. He would be most friendly to me, he would always look at me as if we were silent friends, he would even walk with me and Grandfather at times, but he never spoke to me.

"Guisso? Why are you here? What is happening?" The curiosity was stirring me from my sleepiness.

"You are to go to your grandfather's quarters, Malidoma. You are to speak with your brother." My brother? How did Guisso know that Grandfather was my brother?

"Where is my father?" Father usually made sure that I was taken care of before I would begin my day with Grandfather.

"Your father is not here. He has gone to see the white priest on the hill."

"Why, Guisso?"

"It is not important right now. Go see your Grandfather." A comforting smile softened his somber face. Grandfather had never allowed me to go into his quarters. Never. What was so special about now?

"Come in, Malidoma," came the weak voice of Grandfather as I kept tapping on his hut. Not knowing what to expect, I stuck just my head in to see this place of mystery. I could see nothing in the darkness. It was as if Grandfather were living inside a bottomless pit. So I decided to follow the sound of his voice.

As I stood in the blackness wondering what I was doing here, I could smell the many odors of herbs and potions and roots. As my eyes gradually adjusted to the lack of light, I could see many gourds hanging from the ceiling. There seemed to be a small hole in the top of the dome to which all the containers seemed to be tied or connected. It looked like a road map made of rope that led to all the medicines.

"Come here, Malidoma," came Grandfather's voice once again. I could not see where he was. So once again I moved to where I thought the voice was coming from. I stumbled on a rise of dirt and fell into a pile of humanity. It was Grandfather, lying on his bed of mud with a sand pillow beneath his head. "You have not been here before, have you?"

"No, Grandfather, you would not allow me in here." I could now make out his eyes as they stared straight up to the ceiling. His breathing was brief but calm.

"That is because you were not to see what you now see until you were initiated or until I was to travel to the Otherworld. There are things that I wish to tell you. Sit closely to me."

I scooted as close as I could without taking more space away from an already sparse bed of hardened mud. It was a while until he spoke again. "You are Malidoma, 'be friend with the enemy.' You are of the house of Birifor, we who are priests with the Otherworld." I was not prepared for what Grandfather had to tell me. I held his hand tightly as he talked on and on about the family history, about the courageous war against the white man. How the upside-down arrow hit its mark at night, killing the enemy without a blow. How the white man's machines won the battles by day, but the Dagara won the battles by night, when the arrows of the Otherworld were delivered. He told how the war ended when one of the white priests was seen giving aid to the women of the village who had been hidden from the zone of battle. He spoke with great sadness as he described how Dagara law forbade hurting anyone unless they were trying to hurt you. It was not the white man's weapons of destruction that defeated the Dagara. It was his kindness, or so it seemed — the kindness of one man.

"Malidoma, the time will come when you will be only part Dagara. You will learn the white man's ways. There will be many trials for you. Be strong. Know that you are Birifor." I jumped as I felt another hand touch my shoulder. It was Guisso. "Brother, you will be taken from your people and will one day return. After you have learned the secrets of Birifor you will then surrender once more to the milky ones. You will walk with men who live in trees that reach to the sky. You will speak to their hearts and you will learn their secrets. You will be the bridge across the great sea between our people and their people."

Grandfather reached out to grasp Guisso's hand and put it in mine. "Guisso, take care of your grandson." I could tell that Grandfather was looking at me. "Malidoma, listen and watch your brother." Grandfather simply folded his hands on top of his chest and breathed no more. The air seemed to stir with feeling. The gourds hanging from the ceiling began to sway to and fro, then violently they began to create a clatter as if applauding the great *boburo*, shaman-priest of the Birifor. They continued their applause as Guisso pulled me from the room.

The brightness of the sun blinded me as Guisso led me to the center of the compound. He sat on the ground with eyes closed, holding me close to him. Though no grief was shown, he was deeply moved. This would be the eventual resting place of the great *boburo*, my brother, Grandfather.

"Is Grandfather dead, Guisso?"

"No, Brother Malidoma. He lives on in me."

How to Ritualize Life

I am called Malidoma, he who is to "be friends with the stranger/enemy." (The word "doma" is used to refer to both meanings. The idea is that a stranger can become an enemy, and so a stranger is sacred because it is the task of him who is not a stranger to turn the potential enemy in the stranger into a friend.) In my many years since the passing of Grandfather, I have suffered greatly and learned greatly in the pursuance of what I see as my calling. Today, I wonder whether my life in exile makes me more of a stranger/enemy than one who would or should be friend, or should it be the other way round? The quest constantly imposing itself upon me has been more a quest for a home in the hearts of people — a thing that I take as a yardstick by which to measure the level of my own comfort — than a desire to efface myself behind the commonality of mechanistic standardization. And the constant questions ghostly looming in my consciousness are what can I tell my brothers and sisters across the great sea? How relevant is a small village in the wilds of Western Africa to the hustle and bustle of Western society? The West is crowded with people who want healing — this much I have been able to notice. There are people who know that somewhere deep within is a living being in serious longing for a peaceful and serene life. These are people who are so dissatisfied with the existing system that they will embrace anything that promises to rescue them from a sense of entrapment. Without real ritual there is only illness. Such illness cannot be healed with pills or drugs or alcohol, or shopping at the mall, or being tranced out many hours a day in front of the TV screen.

I started out in this book with a concern: where does this trouble in modern people come from? Being modern or

Western does not mean being devoid of trouble. I have come to suspect that in the absence of ritual, the soul runs out of its real nourishment, and all kinds of social problems then ensue. I do not want to pretend that I can provide a model for fixing the ills of Western culture. My intentions are much more modest. They are the results of my observations and experiences as a person caught in this culture and alienated by it. From the echoes of my ancestors, I feel I can give some clue as to how to improve that which is in constant decay in this culture. The truth is, I am also trying to make myself feel good by doing that which my own elders commissioned me to do. If my elders have deplored the sweeping effect of modernity, they have also lived in admiration of how effective news from the Otherworld, the primitive world, can help others understand and appreciate themselves better.

I suggest that the road to correcting ills goes through the challenging path of ritual. I suggest that ritual not be simply copied from one civilization to another but simply inspired by some culture still in touch with it. The soul of any man or woman craves for this touchstone to the inner self that puts us back in touch with our primal selves. In Western culture, the closest thing to ritual I have seen is liturgical ceremony, always charged with boredom, and in any case incomplete in what it seeks to accomplish — an intimacy with the Divine. Ceremony is only a component of ritual. Ritual is not just an elegant procession or music that lifts the soul or words that ordain.

To ritualize life, we need to learn how to invoke the spirits or things spiritual into our ceremonies. This means being able to pray out loud, alone. Invocation suggests that we accept the fact that we ourselves don't know how to make things happen the way they should. And thus we seek strength from the spirits or Spirit by recognizing and embracing our weakness. This way, before getting started with any aspect of our lives — travel, a project, a meeting — we first bring the task at hand to the attention of the gods or God, our allies in the Otherworld.

We openly admit to them what we are facing and how overwhelming it is. By ritually putting what we do in the hands of the gods, we make it possible for things to be done better because more than we are involved in its getting done. Also, willingness to surrender the credit of our accomplishments to Spirit puts us in greater alignment with the Universe.

From an aboriginal point of view, no one can accomplish anything who is not in alignment with the gods or with a God. Anything created without the blessings of the gods or God comes loaded with ills. It does not take much time to send a little invocation at the start and at the end of the day. This way everything in between is sanctified or sacred and safer because it has been thrown into the hands of the spirit world. A person's life is ritualized who accepts the fact that everything he or she does is the work of the hands of the Divine. Everyone can do this. Anyone can, before going out in the morning, send a little prayer to the ancestors on the hills or in the river. It takes a word or two, or at most a few sentences. It is private and effective.

Modern communities can benefit from a good sense of ritual if they begin by experimenting with it emotionally. I don't think it is possible to be fully into ritual while one is carrying a load of undelivered emotions. The way you know that your rituals are having a positive effect on you begins with the discovery of how much emotion is pushing you from the inside like a volcano. Those who are able to express their emotions have been, at some point in their lives, in alignment with their own spirits, saints, guides or guardians.

Modernism means unemotionalism, or that which owes emotion to the world. It also means loss of memory of that way of acting that encompasses both the body and the soul. To cleanse the modern world from its unresolved problems of the soul, there ought not to be a Memorial Day but a massive funeral day when everyone is expected to shed tears for the titanic loss wrecked by Progress on people's souls. I have seen and or participated in some aspects of funerals or burial rites on a minuscule scale in this culture. What I saw was how difficult it is for the modern man to shed tears at length, and how everything that is done to encourage tears degenerates into some kind of strange liturgical solemnity that smells of repression or unwillingness to actually do that which is needed for release of deep grief.

I was once part of a grief ritual for Vietnam veterans. I went there bracing myself to face a flood of weeping eyes. A lot of people were there, more than I could count. But instead of an occasion for grieving, it was a ceremony almost similar to that which happens at Arlington Cemetery on Memorial Day. People showed up thinking this was going to be a good idea. They did not come out of a desire to mourn. The setting was beautiful, the lights blinding, the electronic sound system deafening. It felt as if there were an edge of sensationalism, or solemnity, but no communal grief. The candle procession that followed on the wet road leading to the wharf was beautiful and elevating, not mournful. I remember seeing a repressed tear here and there and wondering why people behave as if it is illegal to cry their guts out. The grief ritual for Vietnam vets was in its intent a noble initiative that fell short of being able to pull the vets back home.

This experience led me to wonder whether it was possible to propose giving a Dagara-style funeral. Michael Meade, one of today's leading voices in men's consciousness and awareness — teacher of wisdom, artisan of symbols, metaphors and myth in the stories of humans — has always been in favor of rituals. He encouraged such a ritual at a men's conference. Of course a lot of the details in Dagara funerals were dropped due to the impossibility of applying them. Since nobody was supposed to be dead at the conference, death was symbolized. It was an innovation that worked just the same. What happened was that we contented ourselves with dividing the participants into three groups: the containers, the mourners or grievers, and the singers. The zeal with which people involved themselves was baffling.

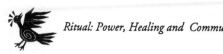

Led by a master drummer, the singers were in ritual preparation long before the actual beginning of the ritual. Over the course of several days, they prayed, rehearsed and prayed again. The grievers were in real grief long before they got the permission to let loose. For three afternoons we gathered, prayed to the waters, the tears of Mother Earth shed so we might live in her lap. We told each other stories of loss, pain and frustration. The sincerity of the tellers authorized the grief of the group. Meanwhile, the containers busied themselves like ants, and with unparalleled dedication erected one of the most startling edifices which was to serve as the shrine and the border between this world and the next. In fact it was not an expensive-looking shrine, just a creative artifact brought to existence by the dedicated wit of its builders. It looked like an arch, or a dome with half of its size being an opening delineating this world and the next. It was made with the elements of nature: dry wood, leaves, grass. There was at the door a little space where, later on, people brought bundles symbolizing their losses. A few feet from it was a line separating the tribe of men from the Otherworld. Twenty feet away, there was a space specifically designated as the village where the grief was supposed to be held. The space in between constituted the road of grief, the place of chaos and commotion. It was made clear that anyone charged with grief should pull away from the village and carry his grief to the threshold and throw it in there, then come back to the village. People had the option to rush to the shrine, walk there or dance their way to it. The speed was a function of the emotional intensity. They were to be assisted by others who were instructed to stop them gently as they reached the line, wait for them to drop their grief into the Otherworld, then return to the village together. Every expression of emotion was supposed to be done facing the shrine.

When the ritual actually began, there was genuineness everywhere. The genuineness quickly translated into an appalling chaos everywhere. First, there were more mourners

than helpers. Loads of them packed themselves up at the shrine. Fascinated by the sight of the Otherworld, they were unwilling to return to the village. Worse, some of them, mesmerized by the beyond, wanted to throw themselves into it as if in serious need to join the dead.

Second, it was impossible to trust that the line of demarcation was going to be observed. The pull of the Otherworld was powerfully visible. The interdiction to cross the line was enforced by guards. They used their fists at times to bounce contorted grieving bodies back to the village. Some people who were asked to return to the village felt hurt. They thought it meant that once again it was not OK to grieve. So they turned around and mourned their way back to the village. I was appalled. Normally, from an indigenous point of view, if you want to know where a funeral shrine is, follow a griever. This time it did not work. How did it happened that the village was turned into a shrine? The implications were so heavy I could barely believe my eyes. Michael and I ran everywhere, like men from the fire department battling a blaze. Someone had to explain in gentle terms to these sincere people the need to avoid throwing their grief at the living. Meanwhile, grievers, torn by a flood of unleashed grief and mortally attracted by the beyond, symbolized by the shrine, attacked the guards who were posted at the threshold to prevent them from jumping into the Great Beyond. They could not resist the pull from the beyond. Honest screaming souls leapt toward the shrine — they had become the bundle. They were recuperated by strong hands and sent back to the village side. As if feeling defied, they gathered their forces together and leapt back only to find themselves reminded in an equal way that they did not belong to the Otherworld yet, and that the village needed them. Other grievers were angry; they ejaculated some insanities at the shrine, screaming at the tops of their voices and ending with a torrential weeping that would break the heart of the toughest CEO. It was no longer a Dagara grief ritual, but a ritual — period. People leapt out of the village in single line and danced their way to the shrine, turned around and came back home to the village. It was beautiful to see. The space between the village and the shrine was busy. The cleansing was happening. So much grief surfaced that the shrine was jam-packed with a crowd of men who did not quite register that they were only supposed to go to the shrine and drop their grief and return to the village where the drumming and the chanting was going on. The containers' job had to be edited a little bit to clean it of its therapistlike influence. Besides these little cultural infiltrations, it was a small success. I saw hot tears flowing from wet eyes. That felt good. I heard sincere groans and yells and screams that almost made me feel like I was home again. The ritual was working.

Even though it was just scratching the surface, the scratch was at least opening something. In a way, there was an invitation to unleash grief. The experience left people empty, light, and — above all — miraculously prone to celebrate. I understood why, in the village, life rotates around grief and celebration. People celebrate because they have paid their dues to the dead. The other side of real grief is real joy. Unfinished grief translates into petty joy and silly amusement. The experience taught me a great deal. Without ritual, humans live in nostalgia.

When there is an opportunity for people to mourn their losses, the horizon for rites that heal will be pure and bright, and healing will come pouring into the souls in a great moment of reunion.

Can I impart to the modern world that which is rooted in the ancestral world? Only time will tell. I offer the tales of Grandfather and Guisso to serve as a testament to what rests in the aboriginal soul. Are we not of a common soul as proposed by modern thinkers such as Jung? If so, then what serves the soul of the Dagara may well prove to resonate in the soul of modern peoples also. And so I offer the prayer to our common ancestors on behalf of those seeking to recover themselves from the rubble of modernity as they seek to work their way toward being elders of the new post-modern tribal order.

> May the spirits of every pertinent direction take notice of their hearts' desire.
> May the forces below pump strength into their feet — that they walk the walk of their life, the walk that heals the wounded truth of their bellies and keeps the eyes of their memory open so they can grow *ni yang maru.*
> May the ancestral fuel burn in their spiritual veins and animate their souls with vision so they can hold hands *ni yang maru.*
> As they walk toward their future,
> May they wake up fast to the dialogue between the soul and the spirit.
> And may they labor to clean the world from its paralyzing epidemic of soul-barrenness so that tomorrow our children can sing *together in peace.*

ECHOES OF THE ANCESTORS

The African Teachings
of the Dagara

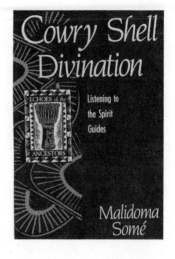

Cowry Shell Divination:
Listening to the Spirit Guides

BY MALIDOMA SOMÉ

Next in the series — Autumn 1994

Each book in the series Echoes of the Ancestors presents an aspect of the Dagara teaching and its application and usefulness to us in our modern Western world.

Malidoma describes his role as Diviner, and how people use the cowry shell process in their daily lives for knowledge, healing and guidance. He explains how the cowry shells operate like "scanners" of energy fields around people and the way in which the spirits are called to the "reading."

Malidoma Somé, spokesman for the Dagara Ancestors, lives in three worlds: the world of his village, the world of the Ancestors and the modern Western world. Holder of two Ph.D.s, he considers his traditional initiation into ancestral knowledge his true education. Told by the elders of his village that the Ancestors wanted him to go to the West, he immersed himself in Western culture. Malidoma now acts as a bridge connecting these three worlds, bringing the teachings of the Ancestors to echo within our own souls.

ISBN 0-9632310-3-0
Paper, 240 pages
Retail $14.95

SWAN·RAVEN & COMPANY
1427 N.W. 23rd Ave., Suite 8
Portland - OR 97210
Fax (503) 274-1044
(800) 488-4849

Cowry Shell Divination:

Listening to the Spirit Guides

FROM THE AFRICAN
TEACHINGS OF THE
DAGARA

ECHOES OF THE
ANCESTORS

About Malidoma Somé

Malidoma Somé was raised in a village in Burkina Faso, West Africa. He is initiated in the ancestral tribal traditions and is a medicine man and diviner in the Dagara pattern. He holds three masters and two Ph.D. degrees from the Sorbonne and Brandeis University. He has taught at the University of Michigan, leads groups throughout the United States and teaches with Robert Bly and Michael Meade at men's conferences.

Each book in the series presents an aspect of the Dagara teaching and its application and usefulness to us in our modern world.

"Malidoma Somé is a remarkable and uniquely talented man. Rarely can one person carry both the ancient ways of tribal Africa and the ways of Western thought and psychology. Malidoma not only carries these, he combines them, separates them, dances with them."

— Michael Meade

Coming in 1994

MEDICINES AND SPIRITUAL
    PRACTICES: Living with the
    Otherworld
TRAVELING TO THE OTHERWORLD:
    Going Through the Gateway

Coming in 1995

INITIATING THE ELDERS: Using the
    Powers from the Ancestors

ELDER LEADERSHIP: A New
    Model for Our Day

Human Robots & Holy Mechanics

Reclaiming Our Souls in a Machine World

BY DAVID T. KYLE

We are trapped in a mechanized consumer-driven society. The corporation-economy creates a Machine culture in which all of us are oilers of our spiritual impoverishment. We have been cut off from the Sacred — the connection with an Otherworld of spiritual reality that comes to us through Nature. Indigenous people and our archaic ancestors hold fundamental beliefs and ways of relating to the physical and non-physical world that we've lost in our society of the Machine. By initiating elder-leaders, establishing epiphanal communities, fasting from the media and mapping the topography of our inner experience, we begin to reclaim from the Machine the Sacred, and conceive a different future for ourselves, our children and our planet.

"This heartfelt book brings important insights, drawn from years of experience, to challenges we will all have to face if we are to move beyond today's corporate culture to a genuinely positive future."

—ROBERT GILMAN

PUBLISHER, *IN-CONTEXT MAGAZINE*

ISBN 0-9632310-0-6
Paper, 300 pages
Retail $14.95

SWAN • RAVEN & COMPANY
1427 N.W. 23rd Ave., Suite 8
Portland - OR 97210
Fax (503) 274-1044
(800) 488-4849

Human Robots & Holy Mechanics

Reclaiming Our Souls
in a Machine World

About David T. Kyle

David T. Kyle, Ph.D. has taught and consulted with organizations throughout the world. He works with Sacred teachings in men's groups and explores the psychological and spiritual traditions of community in many types of settings. He is a lover of high, wild places and lives with his partner, Patt in the Pacific Northwest.

"The society we now live in once existed in our ancestor's imaginations. They dreamed of a world like ours where (at least in Western cultures) the average citizen can live in a manner even an ancient king could no have afforded. . . . Very few of our ancestors foresaw the shadow side of our miraculous culture: the pollution, the regimentation, the alienation, the reductionism which, as David Kyle points out all make up the unhealthy aspects of the Machine. . . . David's book gives us insights and strategies that enable us to stand in that place [of balance and knowing]. It is a powerful contribution in the growing literature of liberation and transformation that both enriches and challenges our culture and ourselves."

— DAVID SPANGLER
AUTHOR OF *EMERGENCE: THE REBIRTH OF THE SACRED*
AND *RE-IMAGINATION OF THE WORLD*

When Sleeping Beauty Wakes Up

A Woman's Tale of Healing the Immune System and Awakening the Feminine

BY PAT LIND-KYLE

When Sleeping Beauty Wakes Up is the story of a near-death journey of emotional healing and spiritual awakening through a long illness with Chronic Fatigue Syndrome. By going through a life and death process, the author uncovered a new path to a woman's feminine strength and discovered a simple healing system. Her research with professional women presents the loss of true feminine experience in our culture and how women can return to an inward presence to have stronger self-esteem, self-image and knowledge of the transforming feminine.

"Hers is not only a literal story of her battle with a 'woman's disease' but also a metaphorical telling about the condition of many American women today, whose efforts toward healing are really attempts to reclaim their power in a subtly but insidiously male-dominated culture."

— Laurie Wimmer
Executive Director
Oregon Commission on Women

ISBN 0-9632310-3-0
Paper, 256 pages
Retail $14.95

SWAN•RAVEN & COMPANY
1427 N.W. 23rd Ave., Suite 8
Portland - OR 97210
Fax (503) 274-1044
(800) 488-4849

When Sleeping Beauty Wakes Up

A Woman's Tale of Healing
the Immune System and
Awakening the Feminine

About Patt Lind-Kyle

Patt Lind-Kyle is a psychologist who has taught and consulted in the business community and has a private practice whose focus is with professional women. She received a B.S. in biology from the University of Southern California and an M.A. in psychology from the California Institute of Integral Studies. She is founder of the Swan Institute for the Emerging Woman Leader.

Patt Lind-Kyle lectures widely, gives seminars to women's groups, and appears at Chronic Fatigue Syndrome symposiums presenting the themes of her book. Patt gives a unique and refreshing presentation on awakening women to the feminine perspective in order to understand how they live and work in a man's world and how it affects their health, relationships, career and self-esteem. Patt uses song, vignettes and storytelling in per presentations and encourages group participation.

"In this book, the author intimately shares her healing journey with us, leading us down through the Seven States of Death, to emerge through the Seven States of Rebirth. In the end she provides a structure for seeing ourselves — a clear and simple system to map out our own healing paths. There is pain in these pages. But above al,l this is a testimony to the healing power of the human spirit."
— Hal Zina Bennet, Ph.D.
Author: *Follow Your Bliss*,
and The *Well Body Book*,

The Swan and the Raven traditionally carry the Sacred Message between the Otherworld and our world. Swan•Raven & Company publishes books whose themes explore this Sacred Message.

If you wish to receive a copy of the latest Swan•Raven & Company catalog and be placed on our mailing list, please send us this card

Name _____ Date _____

Address _____

City _____ State _____ Zip _____

Country _____

Swan • Raven & Company

1427 NW 23rd Ave.

Suite 8

Portland - OR   97210

The Swan and the Raven traditionally carry the Sacred Message between the Otherworld and our world. Swan•Raven & Company publishes books whose themes explore this Sacred Message.

If you wish to receive a copy of the latest Swan•Raven & Company catalog and be placed on our mailing list, please send us this card

Name _____ Date _____

Address _____

City _____ State _____ Zip _____

Country _____

Swan • Raven & Company

1427 NW 23rd Ave.

Suite 8

Portland - OR   97210

Place
Stamp
Here